IKIGAI
43 Japanese words to live by

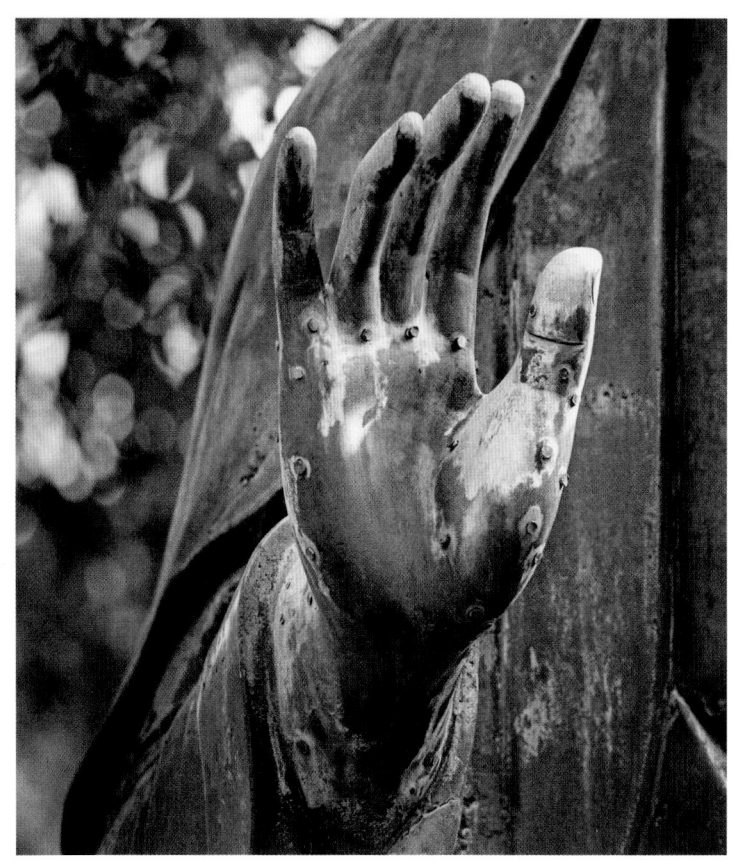

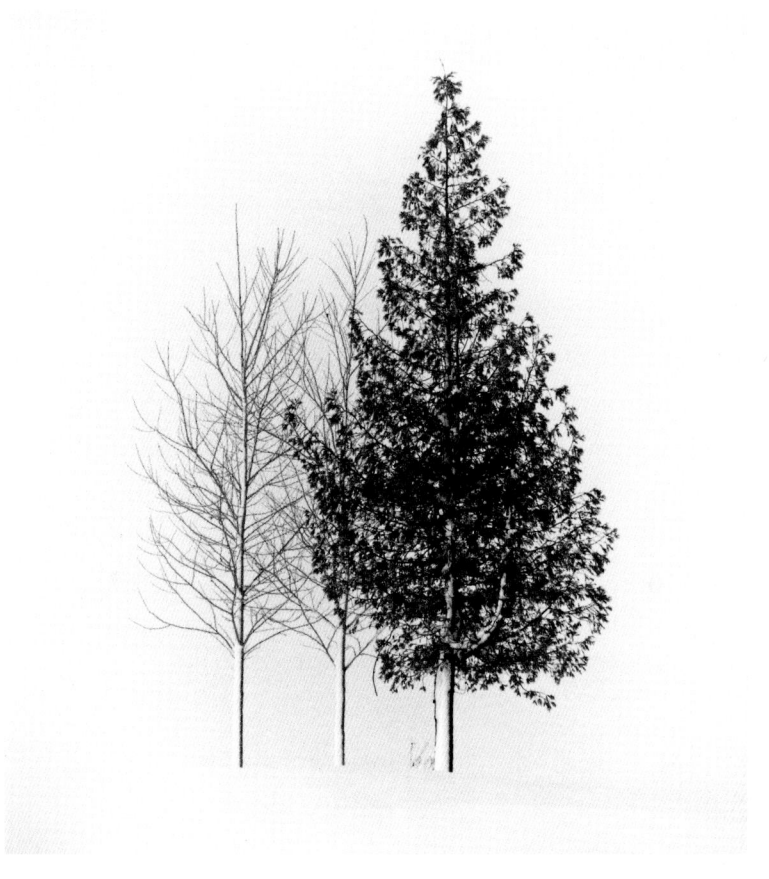

This edition first published in Australia and Great Britain in 2025
by Simon & Schuster (Australia) Pty Limited
Level 4, York Street, Sydney, NSW 2000
Original edition published in 2019 by Modern Books

Sydney New York London Toronto New Delhi
Visit our website at www.simonandschuster.com.au

Copyright © 2024 by Elwin Street Productions Limited
Conceived and produced by Elwin Street Productions Limited
10 Elwin Street,
London, E2 7BU, UK
elwinstreet.com

Additional text by David Buchler

All rights reserved. No part of this publication may be reproduced, stored in a retrieval system, or transmitted in any form or by any means, electronic, mechanical, photocopying, recording or otherwise, without prior permission of the publisher.

 A catalogue record for this book is available from the National Library of Australia

ISBN 9781761631931

10 9 8 7 6 5 4 3 2 1

Printed and bound in China

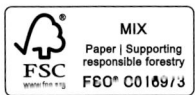

FSC® is a non-profit international organisation established to promote the responsible management of the world's forests. Products carrying the FSC® label are independently certified to assure consumers that they come from forests that are managed to meet the social, economic and ecological needs of present and future generations, and other controlled sources.

IKIGAI

43 Japanese words to live by

Mari Fujimoto

Photographs by Michael Kenna

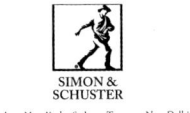

SIMON & SCHUSTER

London · New York · Sydney · Toronto · New Delhi

Contents

Introduction 10

1: Harmony 16
Essay on harmony
Wa a fundamental harmony
Heiwa peace between peoples
Wakei-seijyaku a crafted tranquil moment
Ensō the circle of Zen
Ikebana mindful flower arrangement
Fukinsei poignancy in imbalance

2: Beauty 28
Essay on beauty
Wabi sabi the beauty of imperfection
Utsukushii clarity inspiring deep emotion
Yūgen prizing the mysterious
Shibui beauty enriched by the passing of time
Kanso valuing simplicity

3: Nature 40
Essay on nature
Shizen force of nature
Shinrinyoku forest bathing
Misogi spiritual bathing
Mono-no aware the ephemeral nature of beauty
Hanami watching the cherry blossoms bloom

4: Mindfulness 54
Essay on mindfulness
Ikigai something to live for
Kaizen seeking continuous improvement
Seishin-shūyō self-discovery and self-correction
Dō a path to self-improvement
Katachi a sense of form
Takumi an artisan
Kodawari being fastidious

5: Gratitude 68

Essay on gratitude
Zōtō the gift
Sunao honesty of vision
Shōganai acceptance of events you cannot change
Kotodama spiritual greeting
Amae depending on others
Uchi your own 'insiders'
Isagiyosa egolessness
Hansei self-reflection

6: Time 84

Essay on time
Ichigo ichie once-in-a-lifetime encounter
Hatsu the very first of something
Zazen meditative sitting
Mugon-no gyō the rewards of silence
Enryo thoughtful hesitation
Gaman patience and forbearance

7: Respect 96

Essay on respect
Teinei courtesy expressed through attentiveness
Reigi sahō gestures of respect
Sensei honouring your teachers and elders
Go-on a debt of gratitude
Mottainai not being wasteful
Hotoke remembering the spirit of the dead

List of photographs 111
Word finder 112

surely
  it is spring
in the nameless
      mountains
  a thin haze

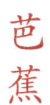

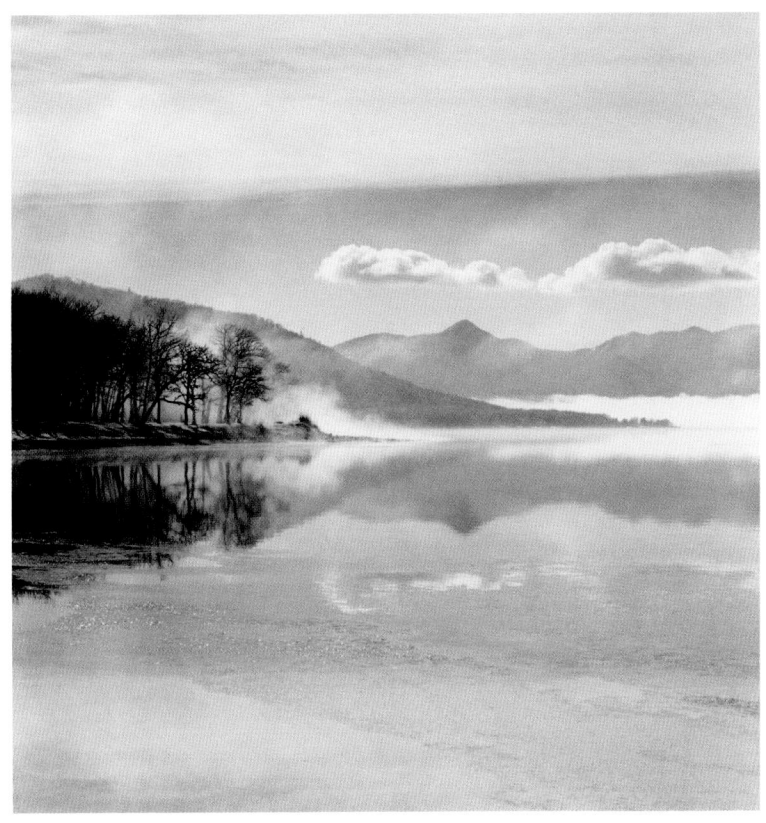

Uncovering Beauty, Truth and Gratitude

I am a linguist by training. I received all of my higher education in New York City, where I now teach Japanese language and culture, but I was born in Tokyo. When I was two, our family moved to a rural town in the Kansai area to be with my father's aging parents. I fondly remember spending *Obon* (お盆), the festival that honours one's ancestors, at my grandparents' house (both of whom were over a hundred years old) with my cousins. We ran around vividly green rice paddy fields that rose to the mountain range at the end of the horizon, dancing under the blinding sun with insect nets in our hands. We had supper prepared by my mum, aunties and grandma: the entire family sat around a huge dining table with plates of big, sliced, red tomatoes; steaming Sukiyaki stew; onion pickles that I never much liked; and cooked rice. Everything was harvested from our farm. This life was inseparable from the nature surrounding us.

Though this rural life was full of wonder, it was not always easy. I recall typhoons destroying the crops and a massive earthquake stole thousands of lives in my prefecture. In Japan, nature has always been both nurturing and destructive. That is how the Japanese developed their way of life: living in harmony with nature, a philosophy that sits at the heart of Shinto, the ancient indigenous spirituality of the Japanese people.

The belief of Shinto is quite simple: everything on earth – rock, tree, river, animal, and human – has spirit. To maintain harmony, people have to co-exist peacefully with a multitude of spirits and be careful not to disturb or anger them, otherwise there will be serious repercussions, such as plagues, natural disasters and death. In other words, keep nature close, treating it with both respect and fear. This belief system developed into a uniquely Japanese way of appreciating beauty today.

How would you define 'beauty'? Is it *The Birth of Venus*, the Notre-Dame in Paris, or perhaps *Girl with a Pearl Earring*? We can all agree that those creations possess essential elements of beauty, such as symmetry, composition, youth and liveliness. We tend to be attracted to those 'positive' qualities, whereas opposing qualities, such as ugliness, imperfection, age and death, are considered distasteful in the Western world. The traditional Japanese aesthetic is, conversely, founded on the undeniable truth of nature; everything in nature is transient; nothing lasts, and nothing is perfect. There is a beauty in all the varied spectra of life, from birth to death, imperfection to perfection, ugliness to elegance.

Now that I live in New York, I find this philosophy more endearing than ever before. These ideas have been a part of Japanese culture for centuries. I believe they give us the potential to see life more authentically. In my lectures, I often discuss how the Japanese culture perceives ideas differently from the Western mindset; there are so many things that I cherish in Japanese culture that I'd like to share, but there is never enough time.

This book is my opportunity to share these ideas with you. It is an invitation to live by Japanese wisdom, and in it you will find over forty carefully chosen words that introduce Japanese values and beliefs. Showing us how we might find meaning and fulfilment through our attitudes to spirituality, beauty and change, these words are our guide to exploring and experiencing a simpler, more mindful approach to our lives. In 'Beauty', you can grow to understand how to find stillness, savouring and appreciating a simple moment. 'Harmony' and 'Mindfulness' are about reflection and self-discovery; you can map a path to personal growth through thoughtful activities that teach the value of self-discipline. 'Respect' describes the ways in which deference and courtesy can strengthen the ties between people and instil a reverence for the natural world.

Although the words are loosely classified into different categories, you may start reading from any part you choose: the concepts presented here are intertwined with one another. And once you complete this book, as you complete a jigsaw puzzle, a whole picture will reveal itself. In this way, I hope that this book be will your first steps towards a more authentic, meaningful and creative life.

I would also like you to enjoy the *haiku* (俳句) that are included throughout the book. These traditional Japanese poems, written by a master poet of the seventeenth century, Matsuo Bashō, evoke emotional intensity within a small and enclosed space – crystallizing a world of feeling in seventeen syllables. Capturing a sense of stillness, beauty and transience, the *haiku* encapsulates many of the ideas that are so central to this book. David Buchler's expressive essay pieces, similarly, dwell on the sensibility of each philosophical concept. His vivid vignettes are included at the beginning of each section, providing a frame for the words that follow. They allow language and philosophy to merge with experience and emotion.

You may notice the various Japanese orthographies included alongside each word. Japanese is mainly written using a combination of *hiragana* (ひらがな) and *kanji* (漢字). Both writing scripts were derived from Chinese characters over 1,000 years ago. *Hiragana* is a phonetic lettering system, similar to an alphabet and distinguished by its curved appearance, that represents sounds in the Japanese language. *Kanji*, on the other hand, is composed of 'ideographs', symbols representing a total idea or an object, rather than the sounds of a word; you will recognize *kanji* by its characters, composed of straight and diagonal lines. I have provided these authentic scripts so that you gain an understanding of the constituent elements of these words and how they mean what they mean.

Living in today's frenetic online world, I often feel disconnected – from reality, from people and from nature. I long for the time I spend with my family during *Obon*. I frequently catch myself worrying about so many things – my family, aging, violence in the world, pretty much everything. I believe that is why it is crucial to keep many of the words in this book close to your heart. We sometimes need to stop what we are doing and bring our attention towards experiencing what is happening around us in the present moment. To be happy with who you are, to find beauty, to discover peace, you must find the spirits around you and keep them close. Japanese people, including myself, tend to believe in *en* (縁), a mysterious force that connects us to others. Meeting people or making a welcome discovery is something that we feel grateful for and appreciate, rather than dismissing as a randomly occurring event. So, I thank you for discovering this book, and uncovering that *en* that we now we share together.

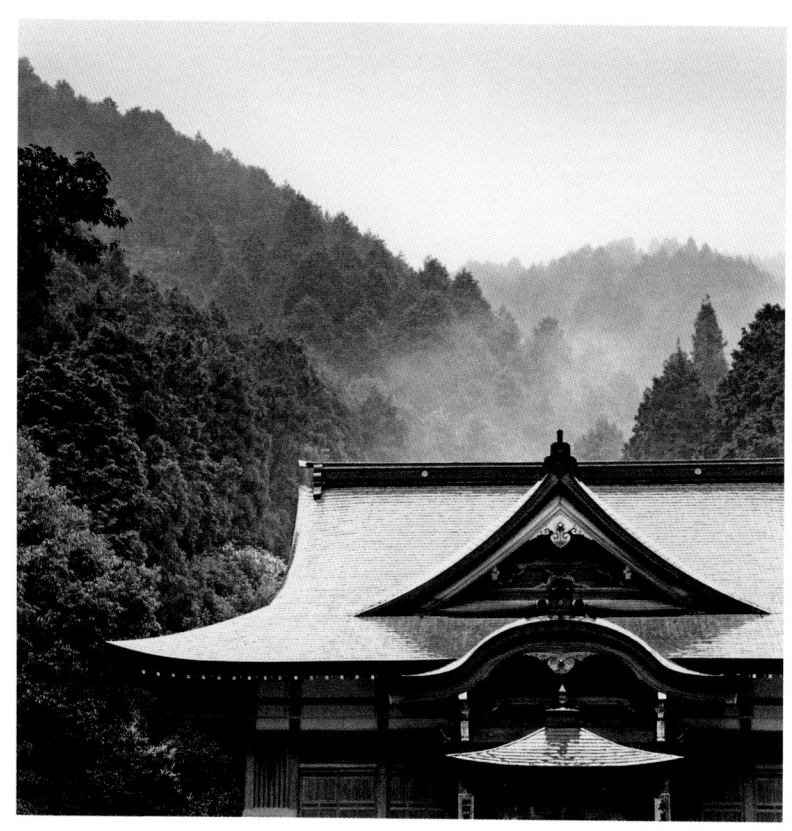

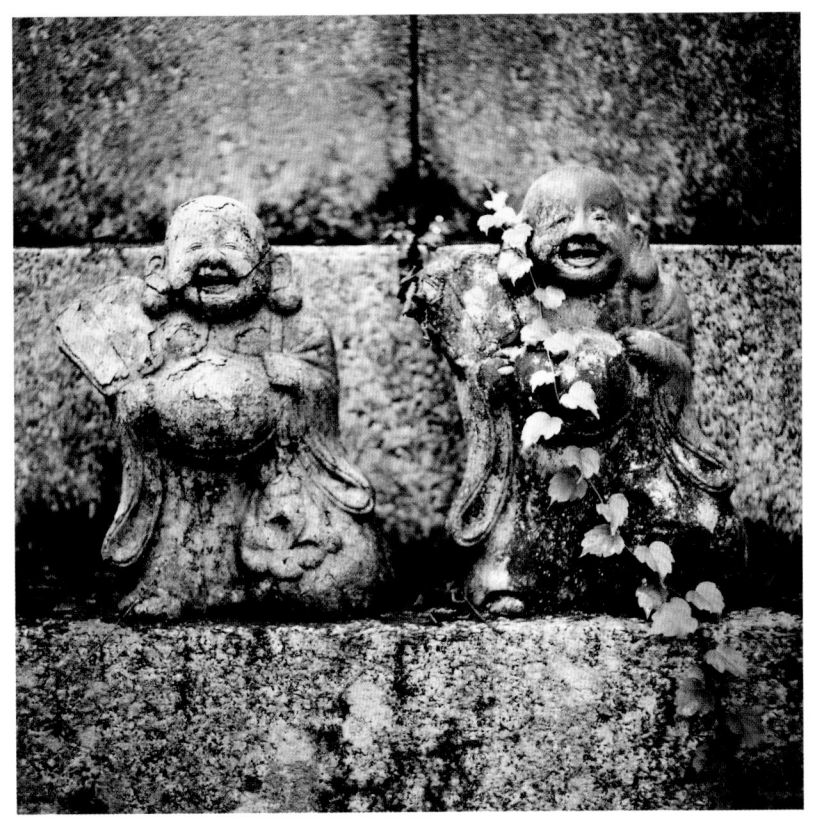

Old pond
a frog
jumps into
the sound
of water

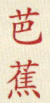

Part 1

Harmony

Concepts of togetherness that find kinship in peace, acceptance and, rather than perfection, asymmetry.

On Harmony

What is nurtured in the dark, *flourishes* in the light.

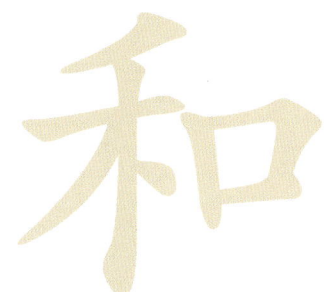

    Just like a plant
    pushing through concrete,
    the nature of this beauty is fostered by challenge.
    A passion to thrive.
    An unfaltering belief
    that there is always room to grow.

    Light diffused through rice paper. The delicate glow.

Seeing through it, but not seeing.

    There is a great Buddha that sits near the ocean in Kamakura. Echoes of Kipling's poem travel through the ages:

    A rusting bulk of bronze and gold,
    so much and scarce so much,
    ye hold the meaning of Kamakura?

This Buddha has become a part of the landscape, tarnished and rusting from the elements. Only a faint trace of gold gleams at the Buddha's ears.

In this transient life this symbol of faith remains a constant, shifting and evolving with time. The gold lustre may have faded, yet it continues to possess an exquisite beauty, in spite of the battering forces of seasons
and hundreds of years.

Imagine for one moment: the analogy of a night sky.
The air is crisp and clear; the heavens dark and free from cloud.

C o n s t e l l a t i o n s
                swirl and glint

a scattering of glitter sparkling and catching the eye
                                  with their radiance.

                                            So many stars
                                              abound
                                        on this clear night.

Now, if you will, imagine one star
at the forefront
its iridescent glow appears more striking.

It is almost centre-stage in this cosmic performance
and yet, had it not been for the billions of stars around it, it might never
have presented so vividly.

It is evening, *izakaya* are filled with salary men, jubilant exclamations of
'*kampai*' emanate from a private room where successes are toasted
and failures expressed.

In this space, the stresses of the day are articulated and erased.

Wa 和

Wa is the fundamental expression of harmony and the peace that this implies. It is an absolute necessity for us to come to peace with what nature brings, from the rice harvest to cyclical natural disasters, such as earthquakes and tsunamis, or even the wars of history. The only way to approach these situations is, instead of fighting and putting your own gain first, to work together, to find and give help within your community for the better good. If we are in a difficult situation, let us remember that we are not alone and find the solution in *wa*.

平和 Heiwa

Where *wa* means peace in a global, almost cosmic sense, *heiwa* is smaller in scope, focused on human relationships and personal disputes. The name for the peace that is achieved between people after a conflict, *heiwa* is 'to bring disputing parties together in reconciliation, achieving calmness by harmonious acts'. Though the steps may be small, we should know that we can partake in *heiwa* in many different ways under very varied circumstances.

Wakei-seijyaku 和敬静寂

The sum of its four individual characters, this word brings together harmony (*wa*), respect (*kei*), purity (*sei*) and tranquillity (*jyaku*) to create a Zen concept of serenity and appreciation. It is about taking the time and care to create a moment of inner calm: to live by *wakei-seijyaku* is to linger, to notice, to be present. The traditional tea ceremony best exemplifies how this quiet, attentive peace might be achieved. The word's four elements translate into a teaching: 'A pure and tranquil mind fosters respect for and appreciation of all people and all nature; hereby we can understand the meaning of harmony.'

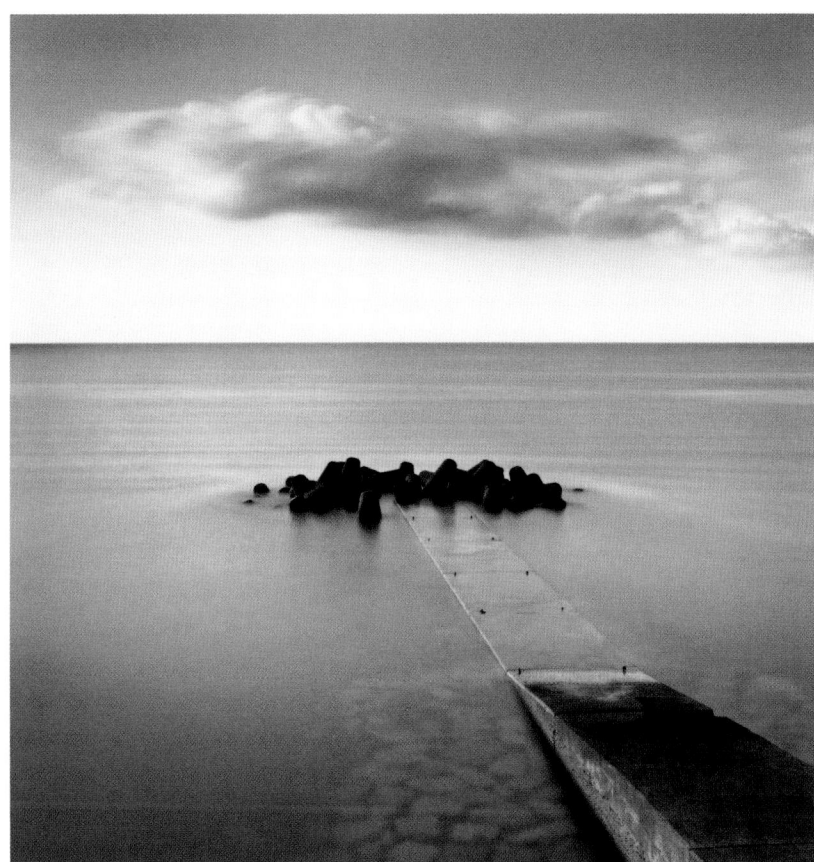

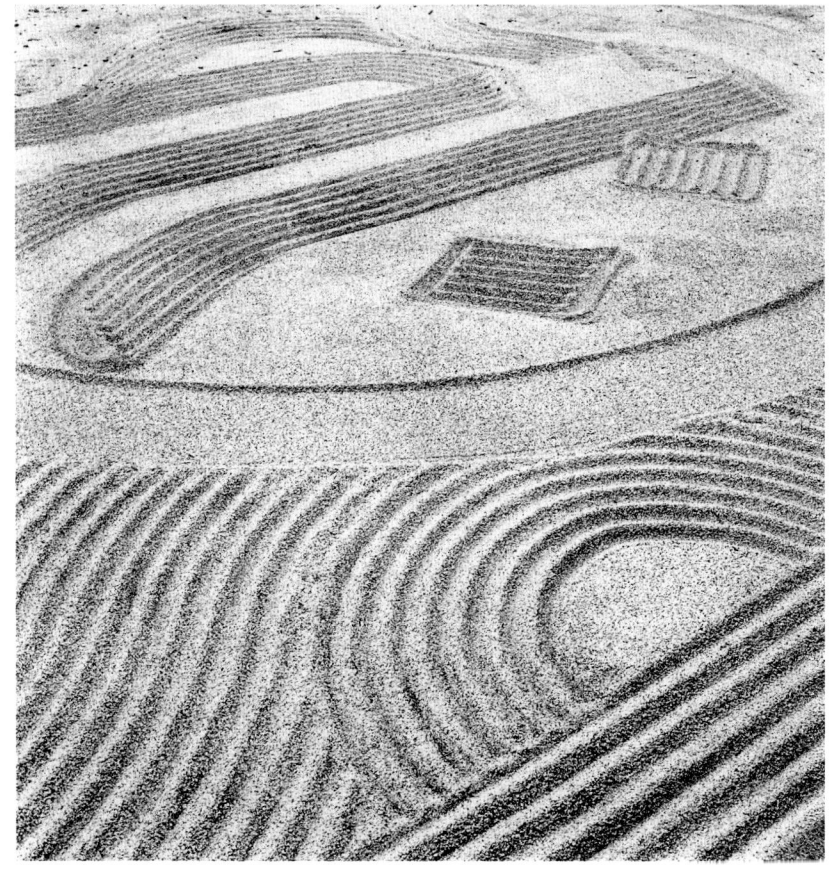

円相 Ensō

A circle drawn in black ink with a single brush stroke; an austere painting, possessing multiple, even infinite, interpretations. The circle may be open or closed, finished or incomplete. Although you might first think the circle represents perfection or enlightenment, the picture has no intended meanings; some see the circle of life in *ensō*. Others see the cosmos, or peace, or reincarnation, or calmness, or even the flat orb of the moon. The painting is so simple that bringing *ensō* to your mind can help you create a moment of tranquillity in your busy everyday life.

Ikebana 生け花

The art of flower arranging is known by two almost interchangeable words in Japan: *kadō* ('the way of the flower', 華道) is the broader term, embodying the awareness that flower-arranging is a mindful practice that leads to self-improvement. We recognize this from the ~*do* comprising this word, which turns any activity into a means of achieving personal growth. *Ikebana*, on the other hand, means 'giving life to flowers'. With the aim of capturing a beautiful and natural asymmetry, *ikebana* creates a space in which the delicate transience of the seasons can be visually acknowledged and appreciated. The constellation of flowers figures birth, growth, decay and reincarnation. Anything in nature can be used: a nameless flower from a field, a tree branch with berries, a withered twig. You can display these arrangements in your home to be always reminded of the beauty of life and nature, and the process of focusing on *ikebana* will train your thoughts and sharpen your self-awareness.

Fukinsei

Symmetry represents perfection, which implies the point of enlightenment or the end of the karmic human lifecycle. This is alien to human experience. An art form must bring a sense of alternative possibilities, admitting change and enshrining the vicissitudes of life; none of this mutability can be delivered beyond a point of ending or state of death. For this reason, we prize *fukinsei*, or beauty in asymmetry. Teacups used in traditional tea ceremonies are asymmetrical and off in number for this reason, and in Japanese flower arrangement (*ikebana*) you similarly position the blooms in asymmetric figurations.

dew
    drips drips
        wanting to
      rinse away
   this dust
     of this world

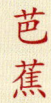

Part 2

Beauty

An appreciation for the elegance of understatement and a sense of reverence for that which is ephemeral.

On Beauty

For a brief moment, there is silence.

 A moment in time and space where what you are feeling transcends any possible explanation or description.

  If it were a thing of Western beauty, you might struggle far less to describe it. You could talk about the philosophy and the concept for hours.

   But this beauty is desolate.
   Embracing an aesthetic so integrated in everyday life
   it is far more complicated to express in words.

 A figure whirs in the centre of Masao Yamamoto's frame, multiplied, blurred. For a brief moment, there is silence. Glowing above her, larger than life, the moon perches on her outstretched hand.

 Its looming luminescence emphasizes her motion, her whirring energy emphasizes its stasis; together they exist in almost perfect harmony, two dissimilar entities contained in the same space.

Such beauty reveals an incredible fragility.

 A director instructs an actress who cannot cry to imagine that moment just before the tears begin.

Stop there.   A holding back.   Just enough.

The space and silence between.

Reading Basho on the train: a life conjured in a few concise lines.
'*Cherry blossoms – lights of years past.*'

The pulsing beauty and simplicity of expression,
the throb in between.

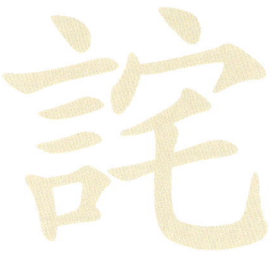

The breath.

    The *pause*.

        The beauty of Bashō's haiku is in the understatement.

    The silence.

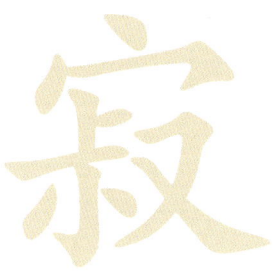

The precipice at the end of each short, sharp line
 where the heart falls

into knowing.

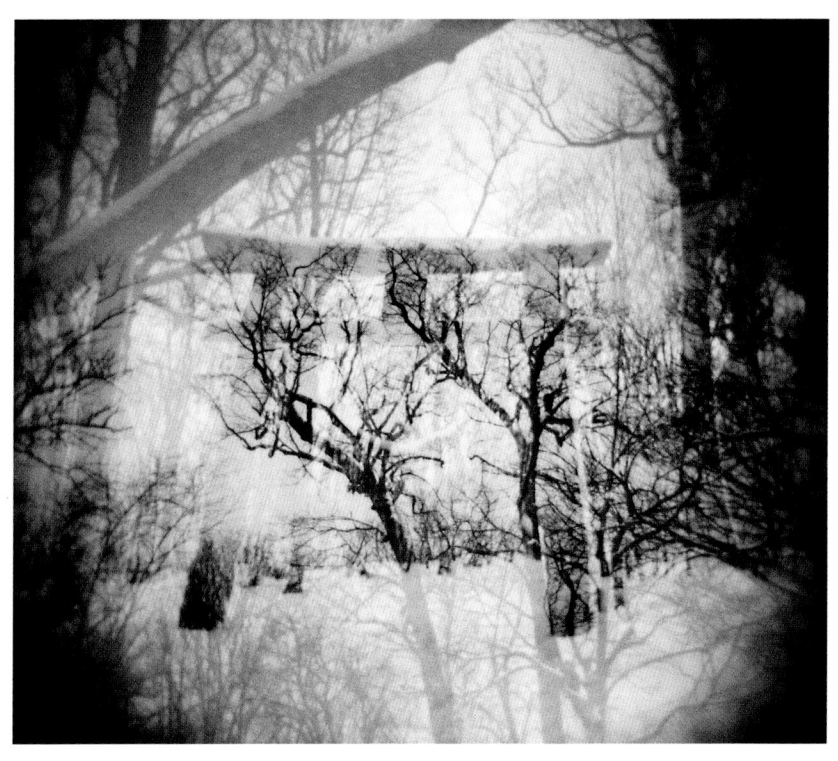

詫
寂 # Wabi sabi

Wabi sabi is founded on the truth of all things living – none are perfect, complete or immortal. The concept takes its meaning from two complementary notions. The first, *wabi*, is an internal process of seeking beauty and fulfilment from deficiency. The second, *sabi*, is the grace found in the decay and deterioration caused by the passage of time. Together, these notions form a sensibility that accepts the ephemeral fate of the living: celebrating transience and honouring those cracks, crevices and other marks that are left behind by time and tender use.

Describing an aesthetic consciousness bound up with feelings of both serenity and loss, *wabi sabi* might be found encapsulated in a simple Japanese garden. Traditionally just a boulder and pebbles, this garden may not be 'beautiful' in the Western sense, but the stillness of the image, the sound of the water implicit in the pebbles, the changing colour and shadows cast by the boulder combine to prompt emotions that are essential *wabi sabi*. Beauty becomes what is fragile and flawed.

Utsukushii 美しい

A beauty that stems from clarity and cleanliness, *kirei* (綺麗) is used when something or someone is elegant: perhaps well organized, well-arranged or colour coordinated. But when a person or object is described as *kirei*, it is not always a compliment, as *kirei* only describes the external beauty. Unless you can at the same time feel *utsukushii* (美しい), signalling a deep emotion inspired by the thing that is *kirei*, this clean beauty is incomplete.

幽玄 Yūgen

Prizing what's mysterious and profound, *yūgen* is a kind of beauty that derives from understatement: beauty intensified by a refusal to state its own subject matter. The renowned poet Matsuo Bashō once wrote 'old pond, a frog jumps into the sound of water'. The spare three lines of his poem express a serene quietness; he describes the faint sound created by a frog instead of discussing quietness directly. The concept of *yūgen* is deeply tied to *kanso*, a reminder to perceive beyond what one sees.

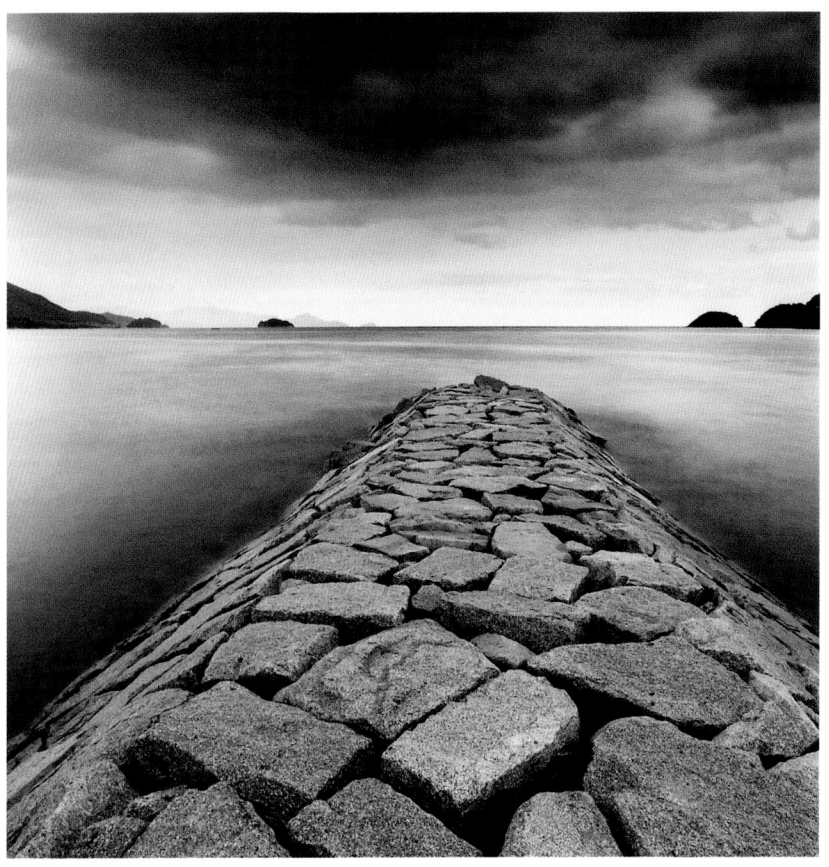

渋い Shibui

Shibui recalls the beauty revealed by the passage of time. Inhering in an aesthetic of calm – colours subdued and brightness muted – this word reminds us to appreciate the things that improve with age. There is a grace in maturity, and the experiences of life mark their objects with a pleasant richness. You might experience *shibui* in the colour of leaves in early winter, or an old teacup on a table…

Kanso 簡素

The two *kanji* comprising *kanso* mean respectively 'simplicity' (*kan*, 簡) and 'undecorated plainness' (*so*, 素). Used as either an adjective or a noun, the concept of *kanso* is a reminder to simplify. Scraping away the debris of unnecessary clutter, eliminating unhelpful habits and limiting wasteful activities, we arrive at a realization of what matters to us the most. As well as a lifestyle choice, this idea finds expression in Japanese art. A Zen garden that is extremely minimalist, styled with only sand and a rock, is purposefully *kanso* in order to stimulate a visitor's imagination beyond what is immediately visible, giving them an opportunity to reflect on important things in their lives.

early

    summer rain

the green

      of a rock

          cypress

    lasting

      how long

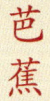

Part 3
—
Nature

A philosophy that treats nature as a source of both wonder and awe, fascination and fear, taking shape in specific rituals.

On Nature

Day. *Soft* still light

Dim winter orb glinting from between the awning of this old tree. Comforting, constant.

Wind *soft* wind

    Gossamer strands glinting, the wrinkling of age, leaves like palimpsests.

      Return,   erase,

            return,   erase,

Sound *soft* sound

The muffled waking before dawn knows itself. Nature isn't silent.

Here, the sway of wild flowers weaved into a silk kimono, a vermillion and violet swathe of questioning heads, primrose and plum blossom. Open faces sunbathe like young girls with no consequence of sun. The bees have gone.

      The world **alive in the stillness.**

Emotion expressed in a flower arrangement positioned in a quiet corner of a house.

The scent of earth, petrichor, damp cold, perfume of dark vegetation, soon the wood fires will be burning. Higanbana will rise straight out of the ground reminding us of the ghosts that haunt the long winter nights.

Here, imbued with memories and melancholy

The season turns its graceful arabesque again and again.

Here, with the shush of leaves, rustling like old love letters or folding origami cranes

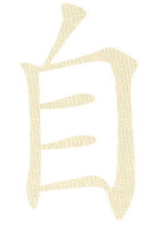

        Here in the solitude

An invitation to be
Just be. The city feels a great distance
The quickening throb of its confusion ebbs away

Soft gentle composition
Blinking colour, a coercion of brightness and decline
The sky . . . blue punctuated with cloud
An exclamation.

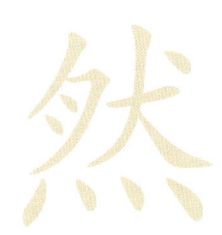

A sentence.

Disconnect the madness of weeks, telephone wires, the Morse code of footsteps, the anxiety and monotony. Moss girls armed with magnifying glasses and microscopic lenses.

    Soft soft landing

S p r a w l i n g space   Breath like peace

        Peace in breath

Recalling the words of Alan Watts:

    'You didn't come into this world. You came out of it, like a wave from the ocean. You are not a stranger here.'

    You are not a stranger *here.*

Shizen 自然

The Japanese word for nature is *shizen*. Moulded by different forces of history and philosophy from our Western concept of nature, *shizen* evokes the beauty of each of the four seasons: the birth of spring, the energy of summer, the withering of autumn and the chill death of winter. The Japanese archipelago is completely surrounded by ocean and the land is predominantly occupied by mountain ranges. In this context, nature has the capacity to be both nurturing and destructive, hence *shizen* maps out a path of utmost awe and respect for the natural world, as well as of appreciation for its vivid blues and greens and its nurturing of organic life.

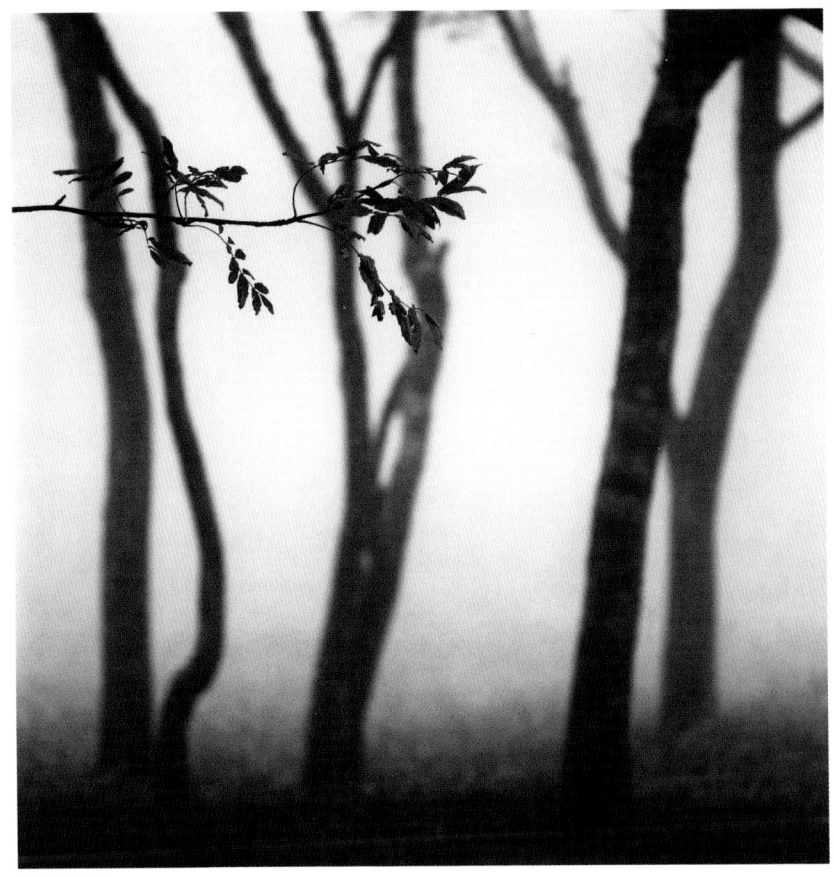

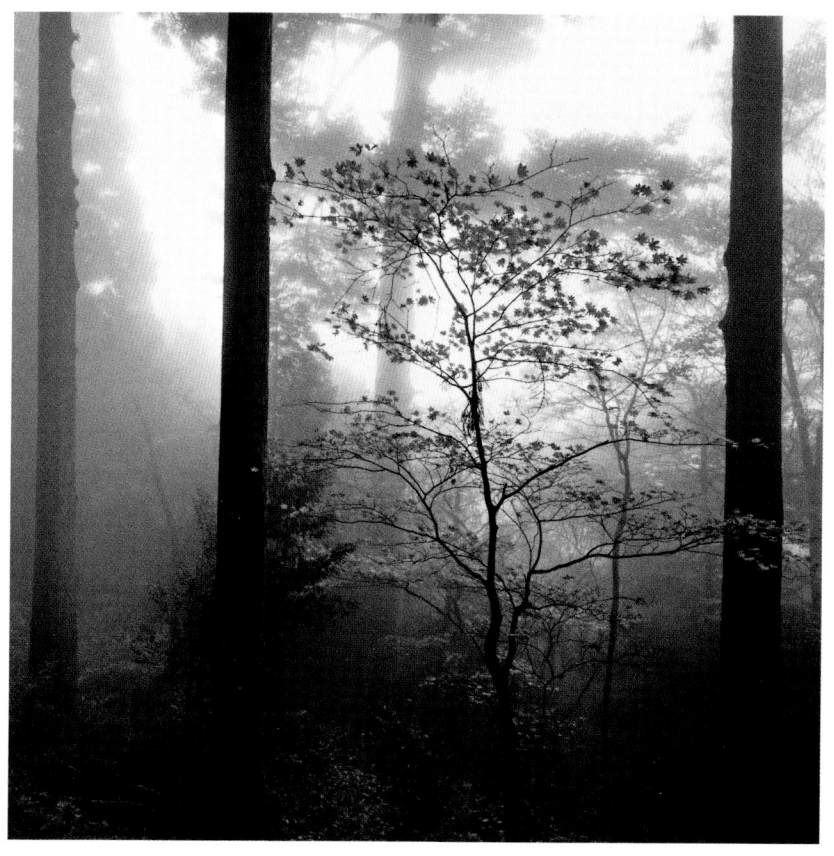

Shinrinyoku

Shinrinyoku is the therapeutic experience of bathing in the atmosphere of a forest: walking through the woods and letting the outdoors soak through your mind and pores. The word itself is a relatively new coinage, proposed by government officials at the Japanese Forest Agency in the 1980s to encourage increased contact with nature. While there are now various outdoor spaces in which you can practise *shinrinyoku*, its origins can be traced to Asakawa Forest in Nagano Prefecture, where cypress trees more than 300 years old enshrine a particular respect for the natural world. Visitors are encouraged to wander in and among these aged trees, absorbing their scents, savouring the stillness of the surroundings and welcoming relaxation into both mind and body.

    Shinrinyoku is practised to reduce stress, to boost the immune system and for its myriad other medically proven health benefits. Yet it is also a fundamentally spiritual experience. Everything in nature possesses spirit; going to the woods is like paying homage to a secret place. People remind themselves how to co-exist with nature, and to respect the earth, by walking through the woods.

Misogi 稔

You may be familiar with the name *onsen*, which means 'hot spring' in Japan and relates to a specific ritual, practised for many hundreds of years, of bathing in the outdoors. Certain rules of etiquette are prescribed: people must strip off all their clothes and wash their body before lowering themselves into the volcanically heated water. But this is cleansing in not only a physical, but also a spiritual sense. The practice has its origins in myth, in which the god Izanagi would undergo the ancient Shinto ritual of bathing: this is *misogi*, a process of washing that purged his body of sins and impurities after returning from the realm of death. Today, the *onsen* itself is believed to have certain healing powers, inherited from the various minerals that have flowed from the earth. Yet it is not necessary to visit an *onsen* to feel some of its spiritual benefits: we can reflect on the rejuvenating power of a soak in hot water. A bath is taken not only to clear away dirt and relax the mind, but is also an opportunity to wash away the day's frustrations and negative feelings. You may then move forward to face the day with renewed perspective.

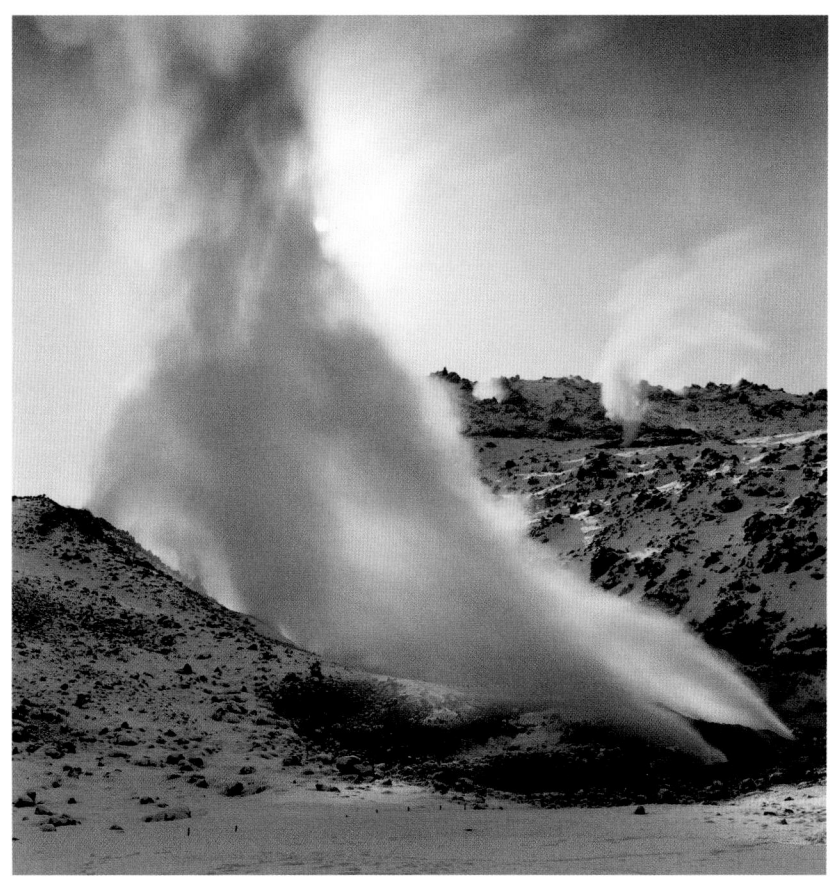

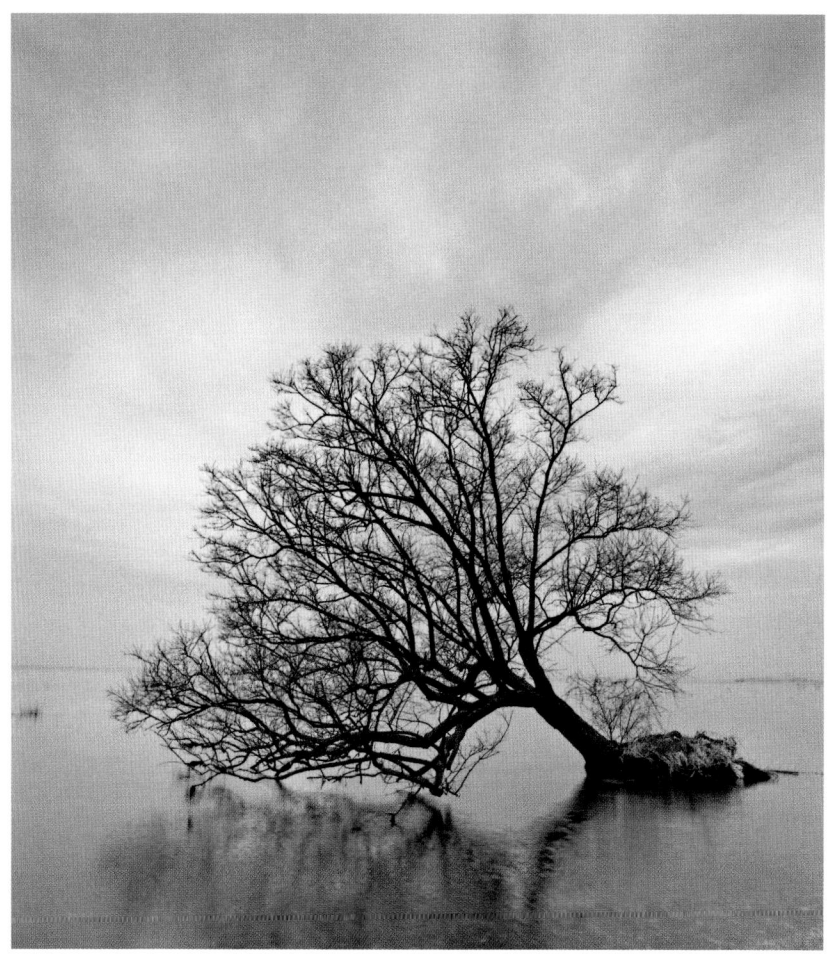

物の哀れ Mono-no aware

Mono-no aware sits at the heart of the Japanese relationship with life and death. This expressive concept is the wisdom of recognizing beauty in each facet of experience, even in what we may perceive as 'negative' in nature and ourselves, such as sorrow, weakness, simplicity, loneliness and death. While we might associate beauty with birth and youth, without their corresponding shadows of age and decay these 'positives' lack brilliance. *Mono-no aware* is being both saddened by and appreciative of transience. It is the quietly elated, bittersweet feeling of having been witness to the dazzling circus of life – even as we watch knowing that none of it can last.

Hanami 花見

Taking a trip to watch the cherry blossoms in full bloom is one of the biggest events in Japan, a ritual described by the word *hanami* (花見), whose *kanji* individually mean 'seeing' (見) and 'flowers' (花), hence 'flower viewing'. As part of this ritual, people gather, sing and dance, enjoying an abundance of food and sake under the trees. What people are really celebrating is *mono-no aware*, or the ephemeral beauty of nature. Knowing that all these petals will soon fall and savouring and enjoying this particular moment in time becomes enriched with significance. People celebrate *yukimi* (雪見, or 'snow viewing') for the same reasons.

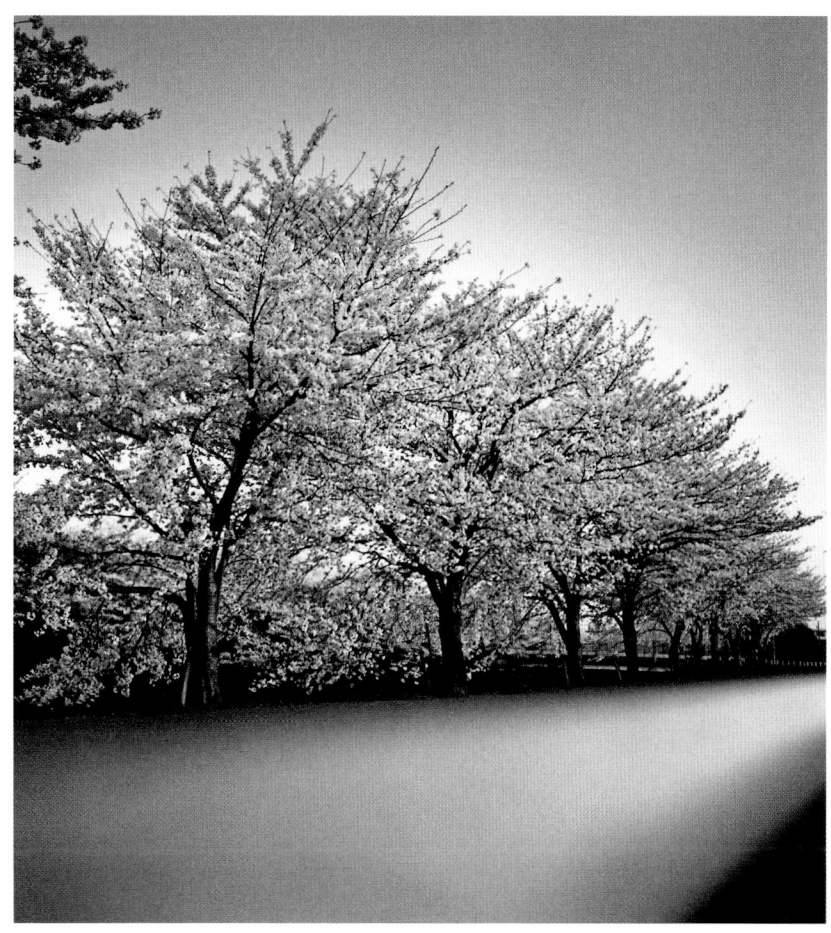

in the middle
of a field
with nothing
to cling to
a skylark
sings

Part 4
—
Mindfulness

Words with which to nourish your potential,
uncover your motivations and
train your attention inwards.

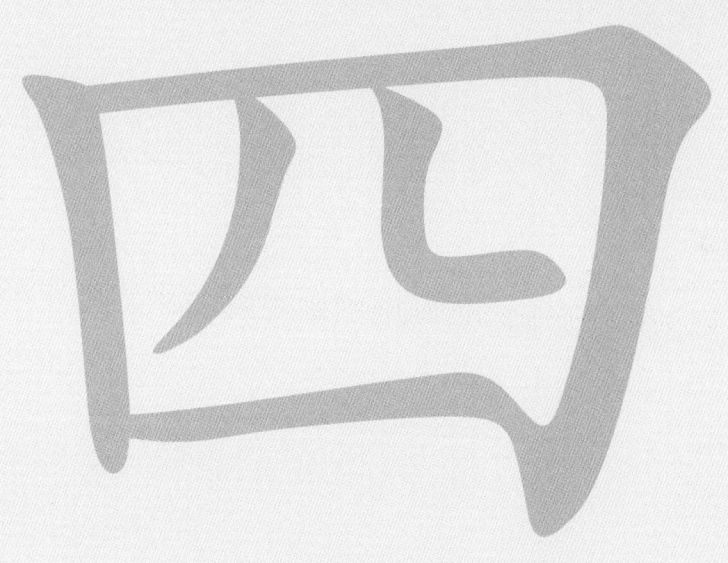

On Mindfulness

Inside a gallery, a large painting hangs alone.
The white of the painting's background has been left untouched.

In the centre, the *ensō*
                or Zen circle is painted in one expressive stroke.

The *sumi:*
        black as the night, bleeding into the paper, trickling like veins.
        Softened edges emerge. It is the nature of the two when
combined.

    The circle is incomplete. The two ends do not meet, symbolizing
    the imperfection that is a part of existence. Learn to remove any
    peripheral noise. Being in the present. The now is where you create
    your past and your future.

Walking home:
        your house. **Broken** roof tiles from too many tremors,

Unoccupied now; no light burns from the window; abandoned and desolate.

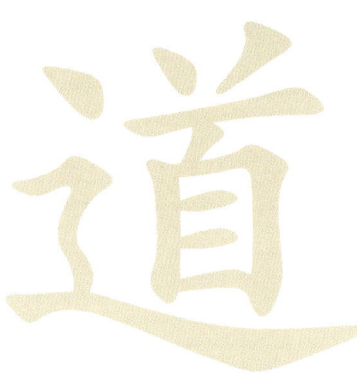

    The flowers in the front garden have long since died from neglect;
a lonesome tree bends in regret, its branches crooked,
yet still adorned with leaves.

  As the sun begins to set,
   the final rays of light catch one solitary persimmon, glowing in burnt orange,
     its wordless haiku
        ## a declaration.

    Through the window, a small room. The *tatami*
               is worn and tattered in places.

Lie down. The warmth of the sun a bath of golden rays.

  Everything is known, familiar. Just as the desolate garden knows spring
  will return, everything that is and has been shall be again.

  This sense of knowing that the elements are too powerful
        to fight or change: in the distance storm clouds roll over.

  As the clouds float by faster,
    the sakura's fragile petals fall from newly opened buds.

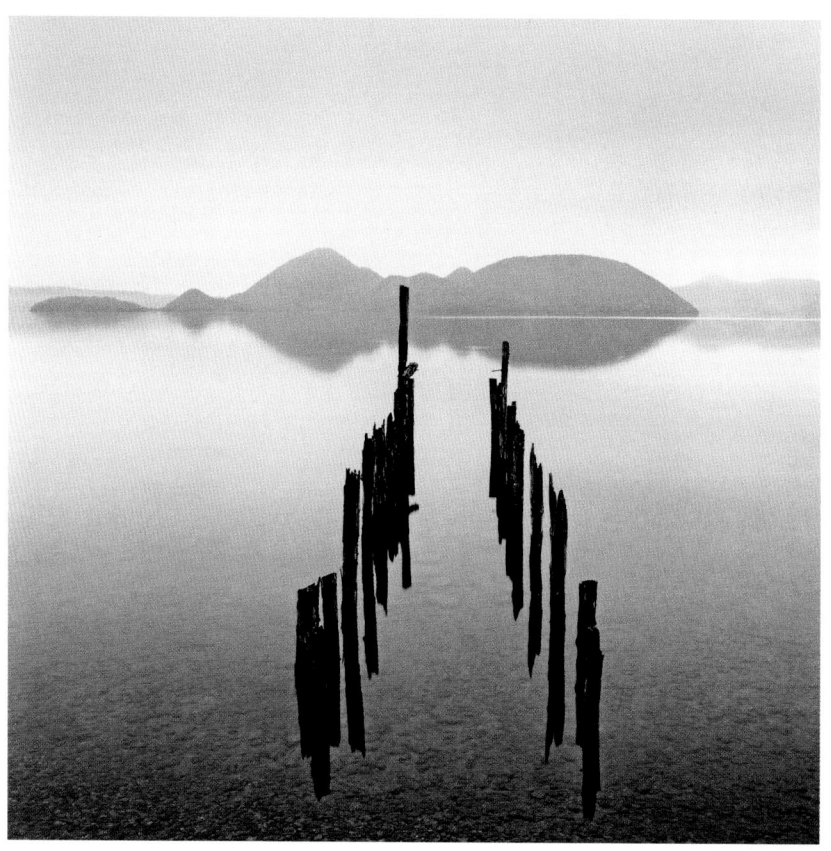

生きがい Ikigai

Some say discovering *ikigai* is the secret to happy longevity. Many of us cope with a life of hustle and bustle: demanding hours at work and seemingly overwhelming family obligations. Yet *ikigai*, or 'something to live for', is the kernel of enjoyment and motivation that gets us up each morning and keeps us going each day. Combining passion, vocation and mission, each person's *ikigai* will be unique: seeking answers to those difficult questions of your feelings and values (What makes you happy? What is important to you?) maps the path to locating your onward momentum in life, and this positive force of fulfilment is subject to flux.

While it may be a lifelong project, to work towards an idea of your *ikigai* is to come to an understanding of what is rewarding and worth focusing on for you, as opposed to those forces that are distracting. *Ikigai* provides a centre for cohesion in this way, and a measure by which to find contentment and balance.

Kaizen 改善

If we find that something is lacking, whether in quality, organization or process, we should take stock of the problems and work to change things for the better. This is *kaizen*, a word inherited from Japanese business philosophy that creates a culture of continuous improvement. Teaching us the value of looking into our lives with the intent to make positive and effective changes, *kaizen* takes into consideration the effect your actions will have on others. At heart, it is an optimistic philosophy that focuses on actions to find improvement. While originally used as a standard for efficiency in business, it holds a personal lesson.

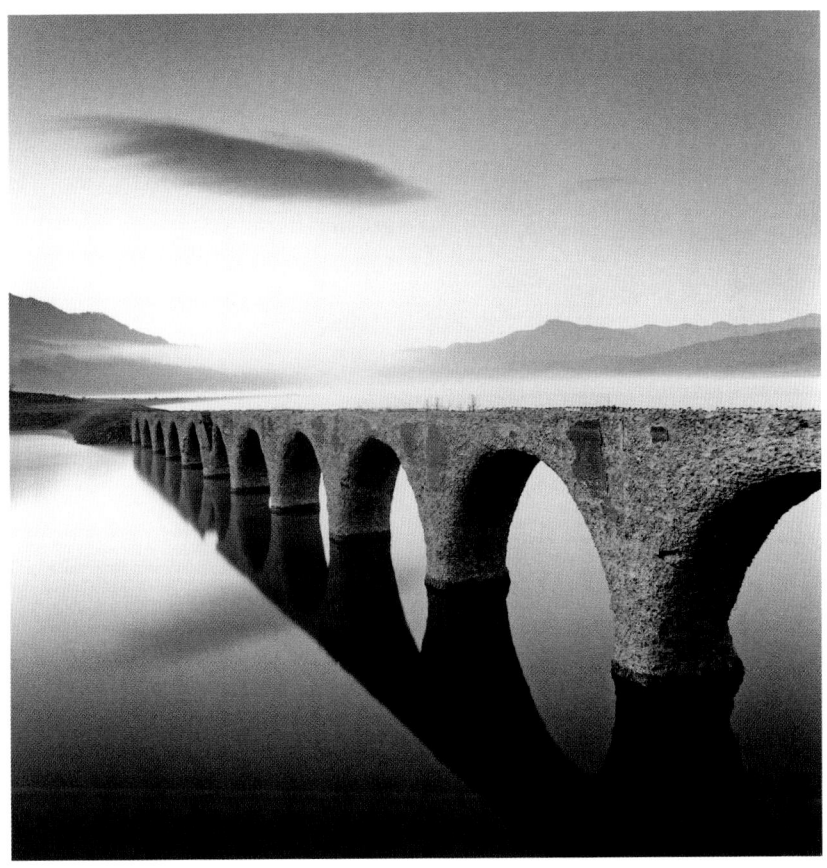

Seishin-shūyō 精神修養

To reach your full potential, you should embrace opportunities for self-examination, self-discovery and self-correction. *Seishin-shūyō* refers to the process and training, whether physical or mental, by which you work towards a goal of self-realization, strengthening your resolve and promoting a robust mind and healthy soul. An ascetic practice, it will help you to take charge of your own life, especially in times of adversity or at fraught points of decision-making when you aren't sure which road to take. You might discover *seishin-shūyō* through meditation, yoga or physical exercise – or any activity considered as a ~*dō* or 'way of' accomplishing something.

道 Dō

To combine ~*dō* with an activity is to signal how that practice, for you, has become a path to self-improvement. Familiar examples in Japan include *budō* (武道), which is 'the way of samurai or martial arts'; *sadō* (茶道), which is 'the way of tea or tea ceremony'; *koodō* (香道), which is 'the way of incense'; and *kadō* (華道), which is 'the way of the flower or flower arrangement'. Anything can be turned into a ~*dō*, however, as long as you aim for excellence in whatever you do. The word embodies your attitude towards an activity: it means turning something into a structured, purposeful exercise that can improve both mind and soul.

Katachi 形

In Japanese, form is something more than the shape of an object: this is *katachi*, which considers the narrative between the outer contours of an object, its purpose and its intended meaning. A guiding principle in design, *katachi* leads to the creation of sensitive, elegant objects across the materials of wood, bamboo, stone and earth, guiding us towards the appreciation of their workmanship and special spirit. *Katachi* does not only relate to the visible, however. As a verb, *katachi nisuru* means to represent or to materialize. And when you talk about a kind act, you might say 'This is the *katachi* of my appreciation', meaning 'This is my way of expressing my appreciation to you.' From this perspective, the word *katachi* can express the direct connection between the beauty in the creator's soul and the object of their craft.

Takumi 匠

A title that signals honour and respect. A *takumi* is an artisan: someone who has dedicated his life to the pursuit of beauty and excellence in a craft. Refusing to be half-hearted in his efforts, the artisan teaches us the value and rewards of commitment. He appreciates his material, elevating the minutest gesture to an art form. We might think how work can be its own reward. To the *takumi*, financial gain is secondary or immaterial.

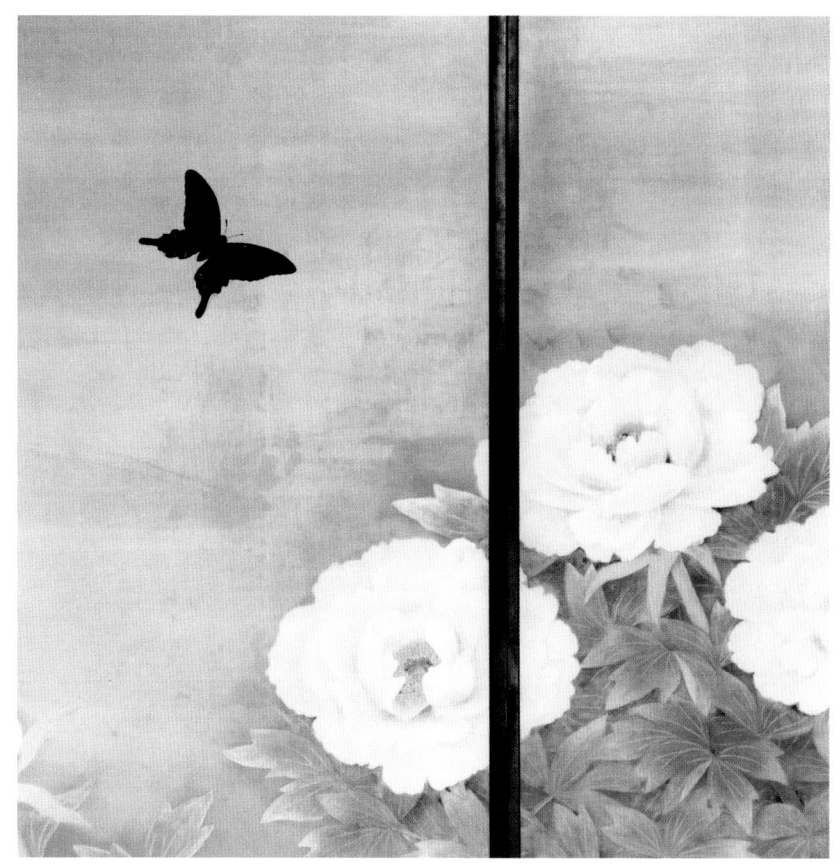

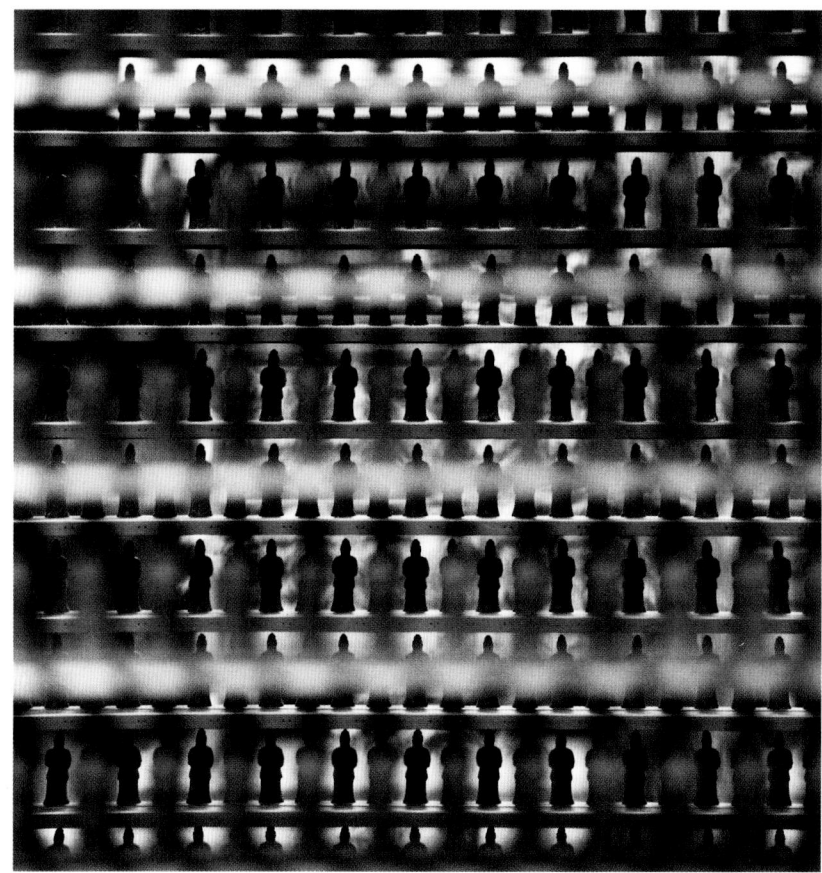

こだわり Kodawari

An approximate translation of *kodawari* would be 'fastidiousness': a mind-set of determined and scrupulous attention to detail. Where this attitude might seem pedantic or demanding, it is motivated by a sincere passion and self-discipline. A true artisan, for example, would go to extraordinary lengths to achieve true beauty in their artwork, even knowing that some of these efforts will be invisible or go unrecognized. The critical attention motivated by *kodawari* is always focused inwards, not outwards: be demanding with regard to your own efforts, not other people.

for these past days

giving thanks to the

flowers

farewell

Part 5

Gratitude

Remind yourself to think of others, to act with thoughtfulness, honesty and humility, and to reward the kindness you have received.

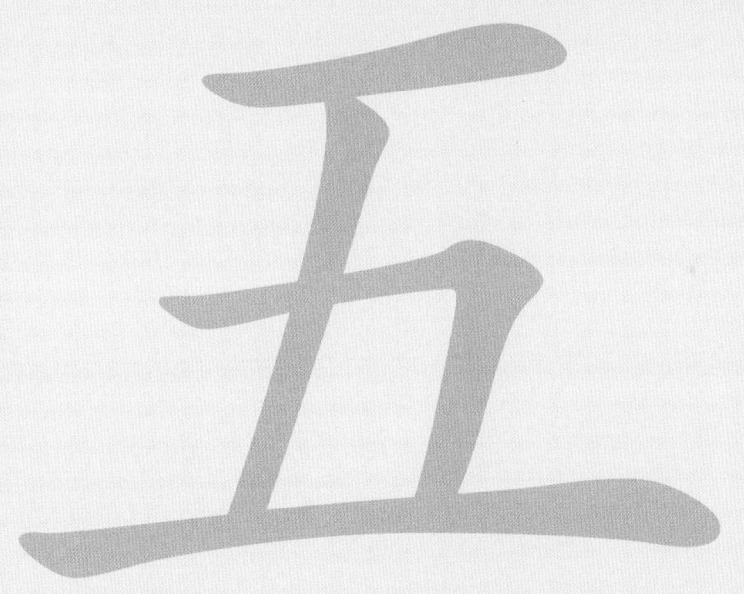

On Gratitude

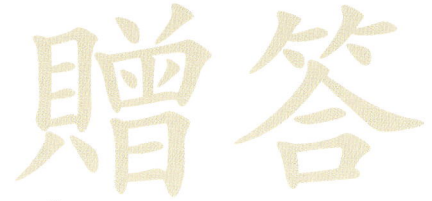

The gift is received only as a gift should be,
with unbridled delight and gratitude,
a flurry of 'thank yous' that continue for much time after.

A package of salty plum tea; a small purse for coins embroidered with deer from Nara… These gifts are an attempt to share an experience with those left at home.

An attempt that says more about your intentions than the actual gift itself.

As the last plate is emptied, the last glass of wine consumed,
then,
and only then,
can we make the offering to the recipient.

The new year.
A single *sen-en* note is folded four times and fits perfectly into the most beautiful hand-printed envelope.

It's a humble offering, given from the heart to a young child at the start of a new year.

Across the city, two co-workers share a celebratory drink. The younger of the two pours the drink for his superior, who immediately returns the favour. This simple gesture of companionship strengthens the spirit of community and respect.

It's about preserving harmony.

Reciprocity: a social echo based on gratitude.

Leafing through an old photo album of celebrations past, you recall the joy of special occasions, birthdays and holidays;
the scents and sounds waft through the ages:

> the songs danced to,
>> the hands held,
>>> the joy and sadness.

That very moment: the day, the month, the year. Sometimes the emotions hardest to fight against are those from the past.

Longing.

Gratitude swells like a warm gold wave: what joy it is to know you, to love you, to share time and space with you.

The guests crouch through a miniature doorway to enter a tearoom. Later, the tea master enters, moving into the space on his knees – these positions help keep us down to earth, and remind us to be thoughtful around others.

Communication and gratitude is a 'felt sense' performed in gesture.

Hands gently pressed together and a quiet '*itadakimasu*',
before lifting the tea bowl to their lips.

Zōtō 贈答

A gift is an embodiment of human connection, gratitude and the wish for a continuing good relationship in the future. In Japan careful rituals of etiquette surround the exchange of such thoughtful objects: a sender will pay extremely close attention to the detail and elegance of their gift, as well to its wrappings. This gift comes accompanied by a special understanding of reciprocity: there is a word for not only the gift that is offered (*zōtō*), but also the gift presented in return (*okaeshi*).

You send gifts not only on the standard occasions of holidays and celebratory events, but also once in summer and winter: these are called respectively *ochūgen* (midsummer gifts) and *oseibo* (end-of-year gifts). They are given to anyone who has helped you, whether in a business or a personal context, in a gesture of your sincere appreciation. When returning home from a trip, there is also *omiyage*, a special kind of souvenir that you present to your friends and family. In this way, we perceive how gift giving needn't be confined to specific calendar events, but can become part and parcel of our everyday interactions. We can think more often about showing a token of our thanks with this nod to thoughtfulness.

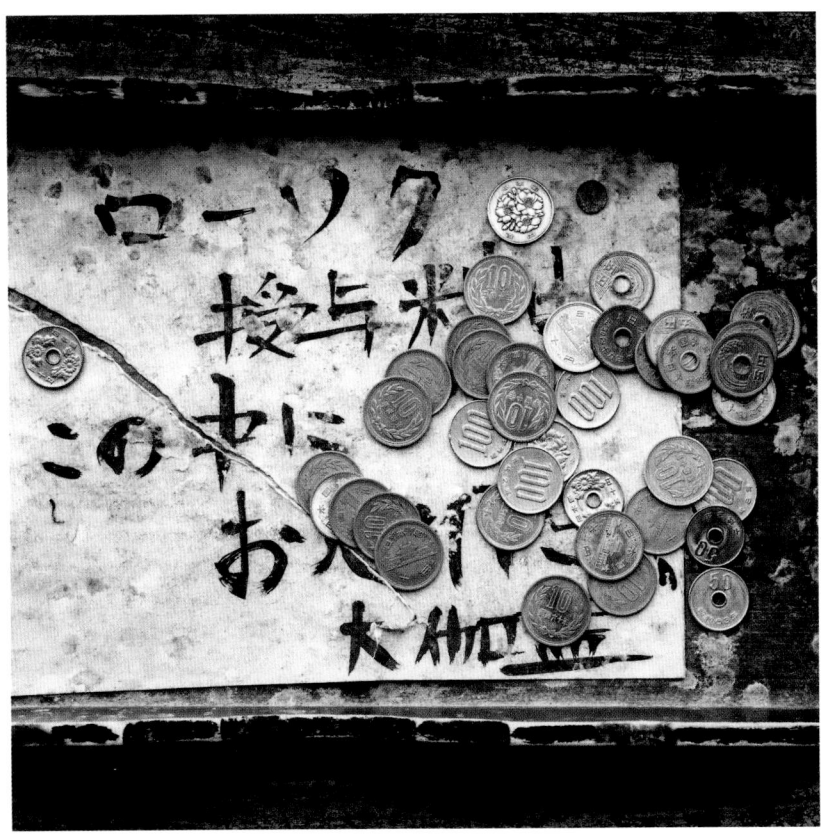

Sunao 素直

Sunao can mean 'obedient', which may sound overbearing, but the original meaning of *sunao* was not so. It dates back to the Shinto tradition of perceiving the world plainly and impartially. In other words, this word denotes a kind of honesty of vision: seeing the world without being influenced by prejudice, being honest with yourself and honest about the world around you. It is a lesson in attentive humility.

Shōganai しょうがない

Meaning literally 'there is no means or method', *shōganai* is a reminder that sometimes we have to accept things as they are. We can't fight change and when we encounter a situation beyond our control, *shōganai* gives us permission to let go of negative feelings, such as anger, disappointment and guilt, and embrace acceptance.

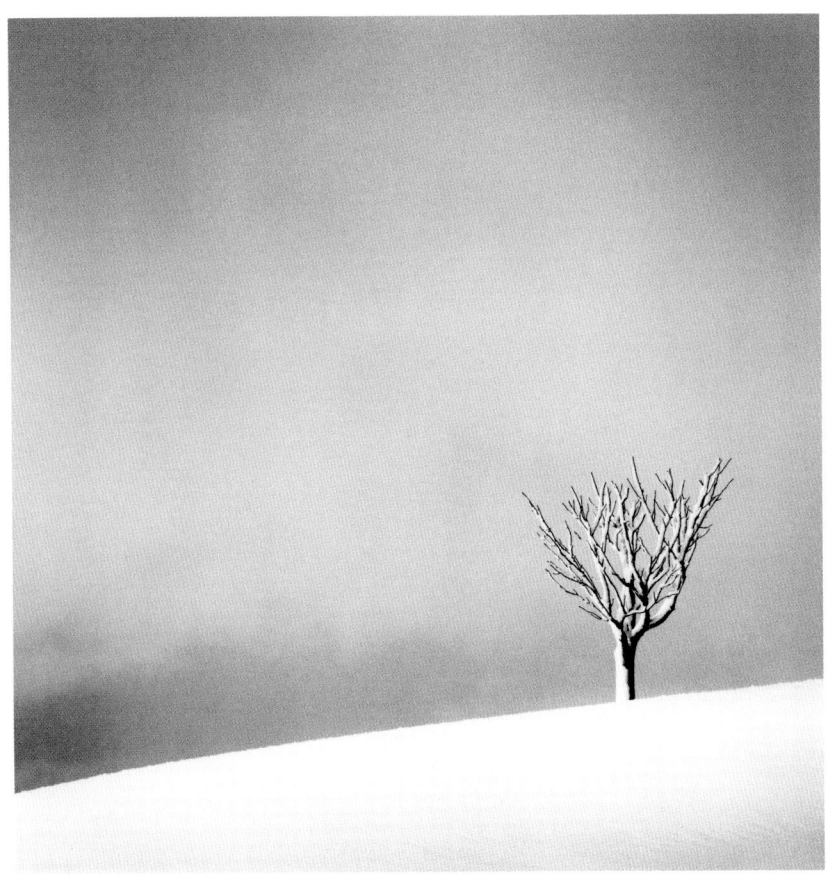

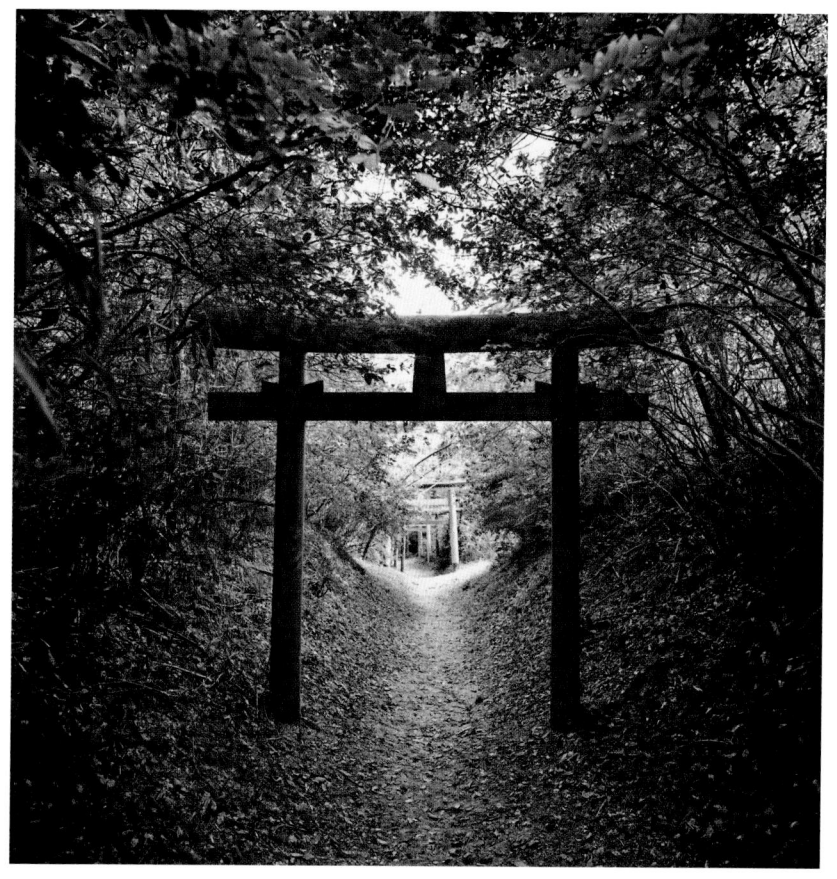

言霊 Kotodama

Commonplace phrases of greeting have an essence of magic in Japan. Many people believe in *kotodama,* words that, spoken aloud, possess an almost spiritual power. Where kind and sincere words bring good fortune, like a kind of prayer, ill-intended words can bring calamity upon yourself. One of the most enchanting of these words is *itterasshai*, which you would say when leaving home. Conveying much more heartfelt emotion than a simple 'bye' or 'see you later', this means, more earnestly, 'go and please come home safely'. Sincere feeling embodied in even simple everyday phrases teaches us we should be more mindful of the opportunity to greet people and wish them well, whether they are strangers or friends.

Amae 甘え

Amae is an important concept for determining a sense of balance in our relationships with others, between dependence and independence, solitude and sociability. In its original context, *amae* describes the dynamic of a very young child depending on his mother – he assumes that she will completely look after him. But when *amae* is used to describe adult relationships, it becomes trickier: if there is too much *amae* this signals an immature relationship, where one person completely depends on another, but also you should be wary of too little *amae* – this implies distance and a lack of intimacy and connection. Since social connection is a human need, we must find the right balance of *amae* to live meaningfully and contentedly with others.

内 Uchi

While it might feel exclusionary to divide people into 'insiders' (*uchi*) and 'outsiders' (*soto*), this concept can teach us how to adapt our behaviour and our language to different groups, all the while maintaining the appropriate level of respect. In Japan, *soto* are always treated with courtesy, even if you wouldn't share your intimate thoughts or doubts with these 'others'. Meanwhile, you should embrace and fully trust those family members and close friends you consider *uchi*, and it can feel like a heartwarming and significant moment when someone crosses the boundary from *soto* to *uchi*, meaning they have gained your trust and friendship.

Isagiyosa 潔さ

In meditation a person aims to achieve a state of composure and 'egolessness', or *isagiyosa*. Literally 'purity', this word denotes a resolute and selfless mindset. The samurai prized *isagiyosa* as a virtue for it allowed their warriors to fight not only courageously, but also without arrogance. Today, egolessness can map out a path to enlightened thinking, allowing us to think through difficult situations with equanimity, and taking a picture bigger than the individual ego into account.

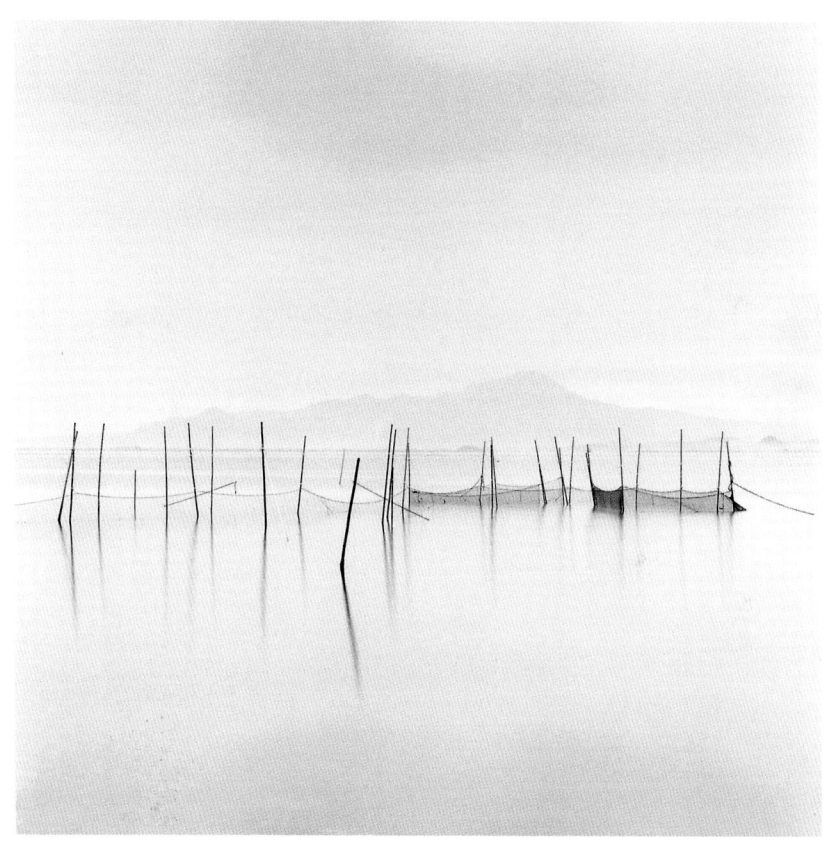

Hansei 反省

Hansei means self-reflection. It has been misconstrued as something negative and reproachful: contemplating what went wrong and ensuring you don't make the same mistake again. The emphasis of *hansei* is, however, not blame but progress: you should not reprimand yourself but search for your next step. *Hansei* is a process of becoming more self-aware, of knowing you have the power to improve yourself and can create positivity from past experience.

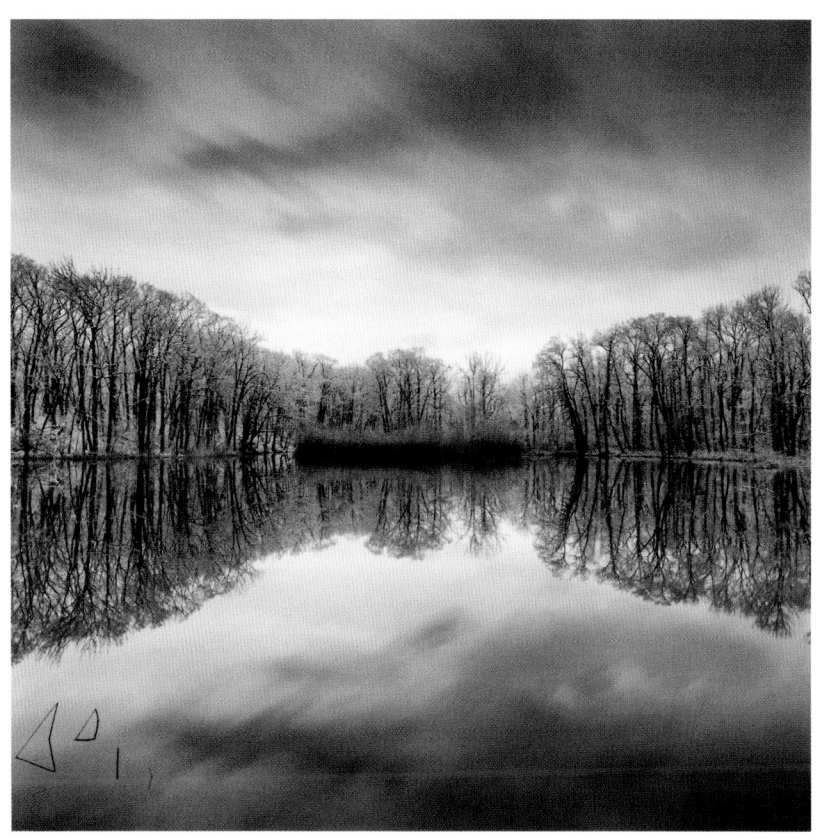

clouds
of fog
quickly
doing their best
to show
one hundred
scenes

Part 6

Time

Concepts that call attention to the rhythms of nature and ask you to cherish the present moment.

On Time

A red lacquer tea container. The surface is worn away, revealing patches of the black undercoat. Still visible on the exterior: snow geese, mid-flight. Depicted forever in motion, migrating and returning.

The snow geese glide regardless, unwrapping gifts.

They arc the sky and will be here tomorrow and next year, as they were here last year. Between there and here, their flight circles in distant folds. Against a red sky their burnished feathers are tinted with gold, faded by the etch of time and those fingertips who have clutched at soothing cups and calming ritual.

You make the tea.
You always make the tea.

Like the snow geese, the nest is built with purpose, never wasted or empty.

Merely waiting to be filled and refilled, dismantled and rebuilt.

A precise spoonful measured and emptied into an inherited pot, imbued with the scent of your mother, and her mother before her, and absorbed by the teapot's inner walls. Suddenly time is tangible and contained in the legacy of memories and forebears.

No pockets to secrete forbidden things
No need to worry if all is known
In advance of meeting each other
For the first time.

                                Shadows of ourselves
                                  Rise out of shadows
                                      Each eye turning
                                To behold and beseech
                                    What is moving fast
                                          And furious
                                To slow down and catch
                                      An endless breath.

This old red tea canister like the pot is engrained with the scent of years. Tea stained and brewing. Everything said and poured. This daily ritual of talk and talk and know and know.

Even now. Still.

Even now with the wisdom of years and the trace of old tea leaves the past remains and is never lost. The same opportunities that exist on one day will reappear on another day.

Wisdom comes from knowing this.

Ichigo ichie

We owe the wisdom of *ichigo ichie* to the renowned tea master Sen-no Rikyū. He reasoned that, while you may be able to repeat a tea ceremony, you will never again have the opportunity to share that moment with the same person in the same way. You should therefore cherish the moment and live it to its fullest. Learn, cry, laugh, enjoy. Treat people with the utmost respect possible and give them your sincere attention – as though each conversation were a once-in-a-lifetime encounter. Never just go through the motions.

初 Hatsu

A word that illustrates how the Japanese see a renewed beginning in routine events, *hatsu* works as a suffix to mark an event as 'the very first of'. So for example, *hatsu hinode* (初日出) is 'the very first sunrise (of the new year)' and *hatsu moode* (初詣) is 'the very first homage to a shrine'. It encourages us not to dwell on the past and to start anew.

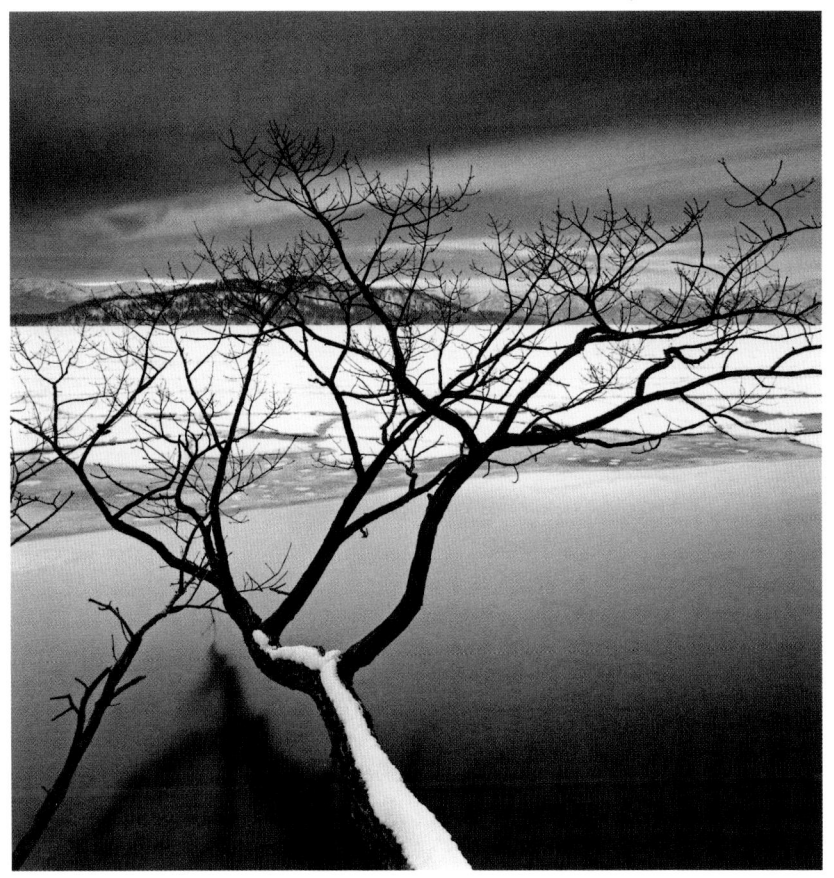

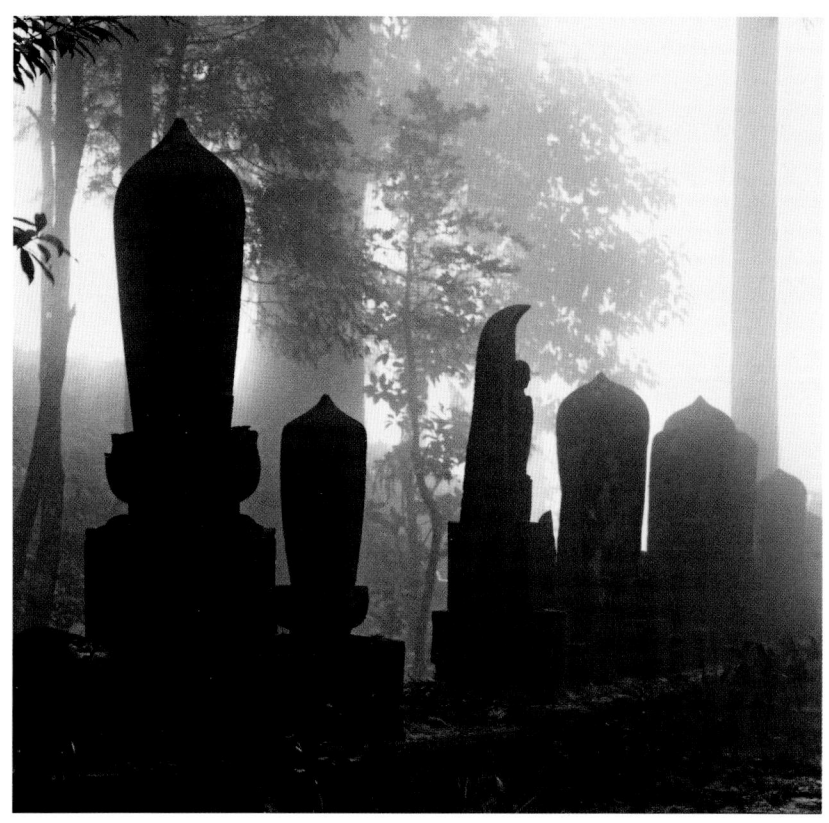

坐禅 Zazen

In a world where we are hounded by distractions, it is straightforward to heal cuts and bruises inflicted on the body but especially difficult to know, in the midst of tumult and confusion, how to mend the mind. *Zazen* is an answer for this: meaning literally 'sitting zen', this is a seated form of meditation. All it requires is a comfortable place to sit, and the purpose of *zazen* is 'just' to sit – to stay and to ponder and to try to reach a state of egolessness, letting your sense of self melt into the surroundings. To do this, you should suspend all judgemental thinking, letting words, images, ideas and thoughts pass by and through you without getting caught up in their complications; focus instead on your body and your breath. You are free to choose how long you wish to practise *zazen*, but Buddhist monks did conceive a unit by which to measure their sitting: an *icchū* (炷) is the time it takes for one stick of incense to burn away. Taking around three-quarters of an hour, this is considered a productive amount of time to sit and let this healing practice refresh your sense of purpose – restoring the potential simplicity of existence.

Mugon-no gyō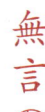

Mugon-no gyō is a specifically silent meditative practice that asks you to take a moment to reflect before doing: act, don't react. Although meditation is often practised silently, the specific challenge of not being allowed to voice your thoughts can heighten the awareness of your motives and wants. By practising *mugon-no gyō* in your daily life you can create an opportunity of pause and reflection before saying or doing something.

遠慮 Enryo

Enryo is a particular kind of hesitation. When asked to give your opinion, make a decision or voice your thoughts, you would practise *enryo* to give yourself a mindful moment for pause: am I about to impose on someone else? A model for modesty and restraint, *enryo* means resisting your impulses and putting others first – taking other people's wishes and feelings into consideration before you go ahead with what you want to do. *Enryo* may be used as a form of politeness with first acquaintances, but also as a form of warm regard among your closest friends.

Gaman 我慢

Gaman is an attitude of forbearance and patience. When we are confronted with unbearable situations, natural disasters and tragedies, *gaman* means accepting these traumas with dignity and without accusation or blame. *Gaman* is of a piece with *ganbari*: both words mean enduring hardship and just doing your best when faced with challenges, until the adversity is finished. Uniting people in distress, these concepts give us the phrase *ganbatte*, which means to express empathy, encouragement and moral support. It's said to people during their struggles to remind them that they are not alone and their hard work has not gone unrecognized.

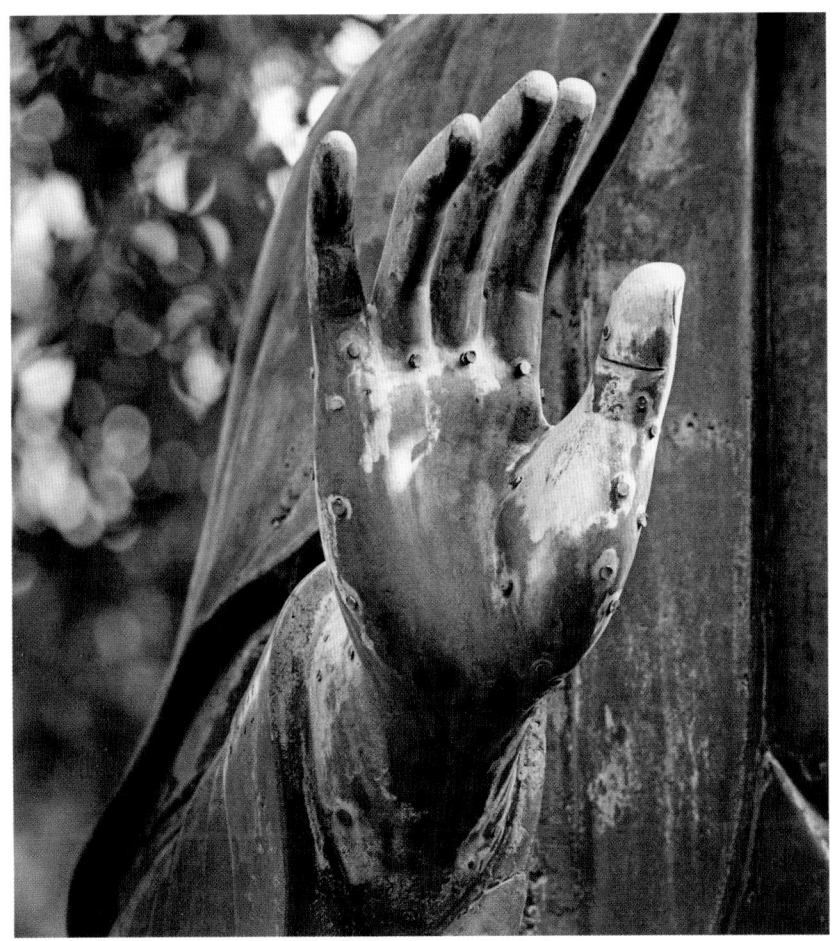

moonrise
　　their hands on their
knees
　　inside at
　　　evening

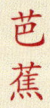

Part 7

Respect

These words instil humility, reverence and remembrance as a guiding philosophy, for the living and the dead.

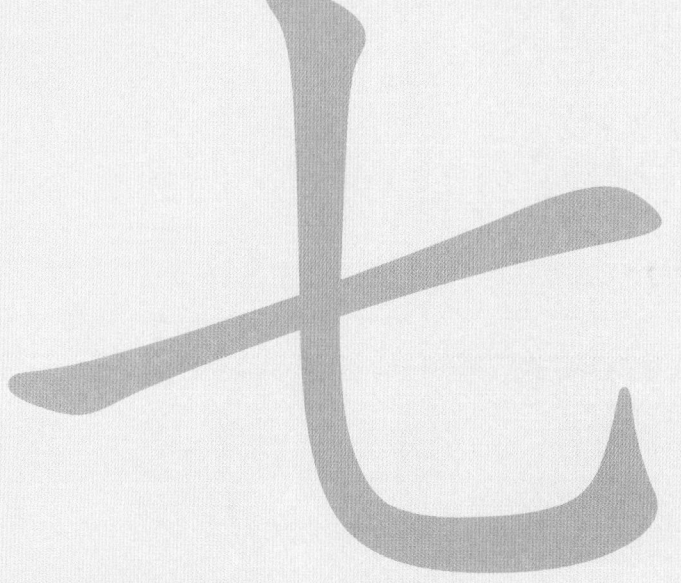

On Respect

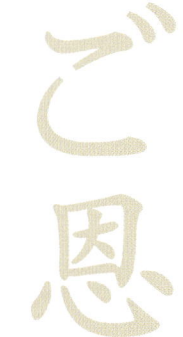

A crowded train at rush hour. Step in
Backwards. Slowly.
Not a word spoken.
Only a slight nod of the head to express apology.

The silence is palpable, respected; it creates space where space does not exist.
Millions of people are involved daily in a choreography
built on consideration for every dancer within it.

A respect that extends like a gust of wind blowing the seasons forward,
like the steady flow and harmony of water.

On the street, four feet apart, a polite bow – the most notable emblem of respect. The angle and length of time creates a coded language of its own.

Understanding that everything is transient, that the present moment is all there is, like the samurai
who had to live admirably and honourably in order to have no regrets when he died,

we seek beauty now.

> *Tomorrow it may be gone in a tomorrow that is not promised.*

Respect is manifest in all facets of life – and it does not belong, not exclusively, to the living. August brings with it the rituals that honour the forebears who have passed, which seek to remember and revere those who gave life, who sacrificed that we may live well. It is through this tangible practice that the dead are not only respected but also coexist within the home, and because they are present and honoured it is imperative
that they are not shamed in any way by the choices we make in our everyday lives.

Respect is a prominent thread in this vast tapestry; it colours all it touches.

> *It is the anchor, the backbone, the rudimentary two step, and it moves effortlessly between all those who honour it.*

Under a bridge, a makeshift dwelling, cardboard boxes form 'homes' for those without one. Conspicuous, they appear like mushrooms, dismantled by morning.

Approaching, one discovers an entrance, covered by a screen of plastic, hardly enough to ward off the elements, just enough space to sleep unseen, and here, at this fragile doorway, a simple declaration of profound respect –

a pair of shoes.

Teinei 丁寧

Tei means 'elaborate' and *nei* 'tranquil', but in combination they become something closer to 'politeness'. This word signals a courteous attitude, where each gesture, even the task of ironing a shirt, is performed with dedication and precision. Where politeness is understood only in the narrow context of manners, *teinei* is a guiding philosophy: rather than acting courteously for the sake of recognition or to show appreciation of others, you behave with the utmost care in order to show excellence in your conduct, paying attention to detail for its own rewards. In other words, doing things with *teinei* becomes an form of self-discipline: an opportunity to train both mind and soul, in the manner of *seishin shūyō*. Making sure to face each daily activity with *teinei* will bring positivity and sincerity to your life.

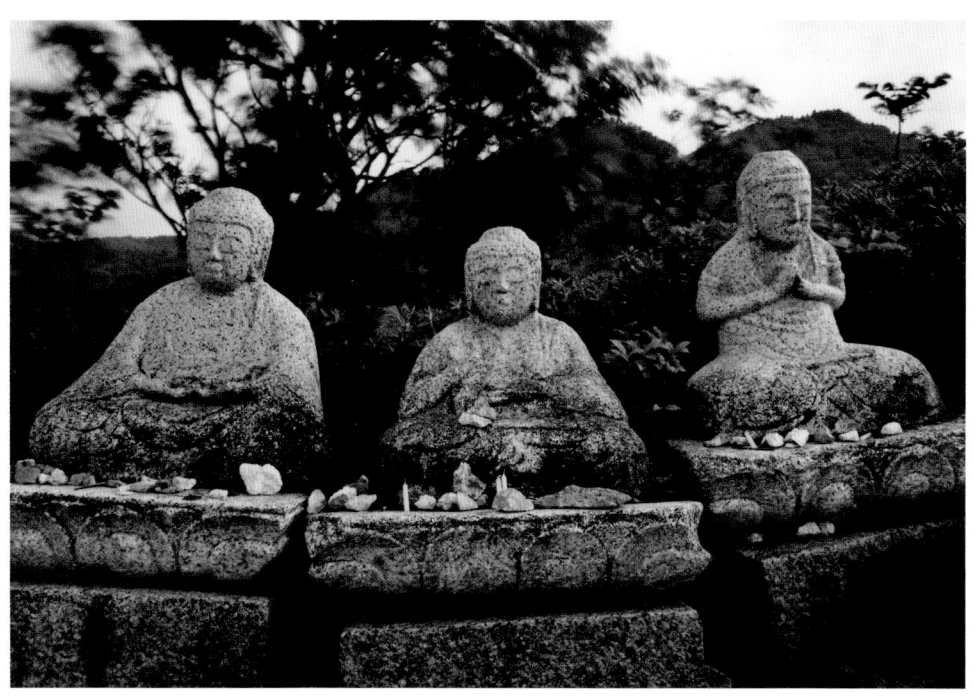

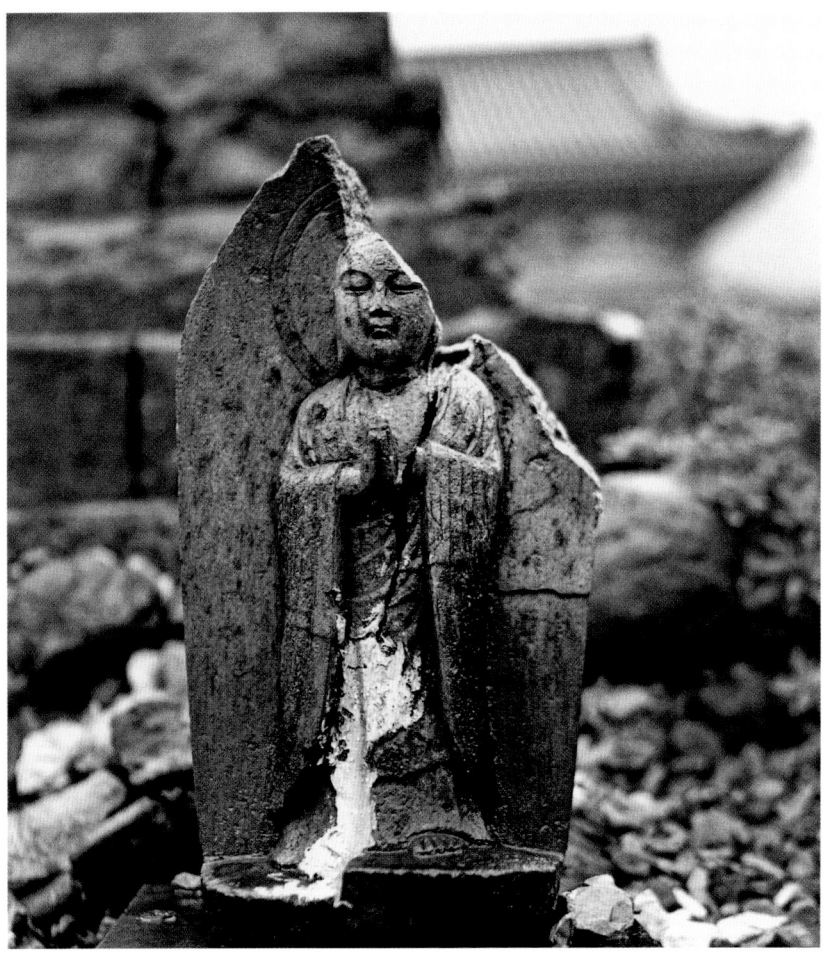

礼
儀
作
法 # Reigi sahō

This phrase translates approximately to 'good manners'. *Reigi sahō* inheres specifically in gesture. It is the manner in which you carry out a task – so, for example, perfecting your speech with elocution lessons, as part of a broader code of respect. From an early age, children are taught to learn and practise such routines as bowing and greeting others properly: this is also *reigi sahō*, which is important for everything that includes ~*dō* (the way of the flower, or *kadō*) or involves interactions with others in a formal setting. It is a system of cultural etiquette whose origins can be traced back to ancient rituals for spirits and ancestors, where the living would express their respect and gratitude through gestures, performed with care and sincerity.

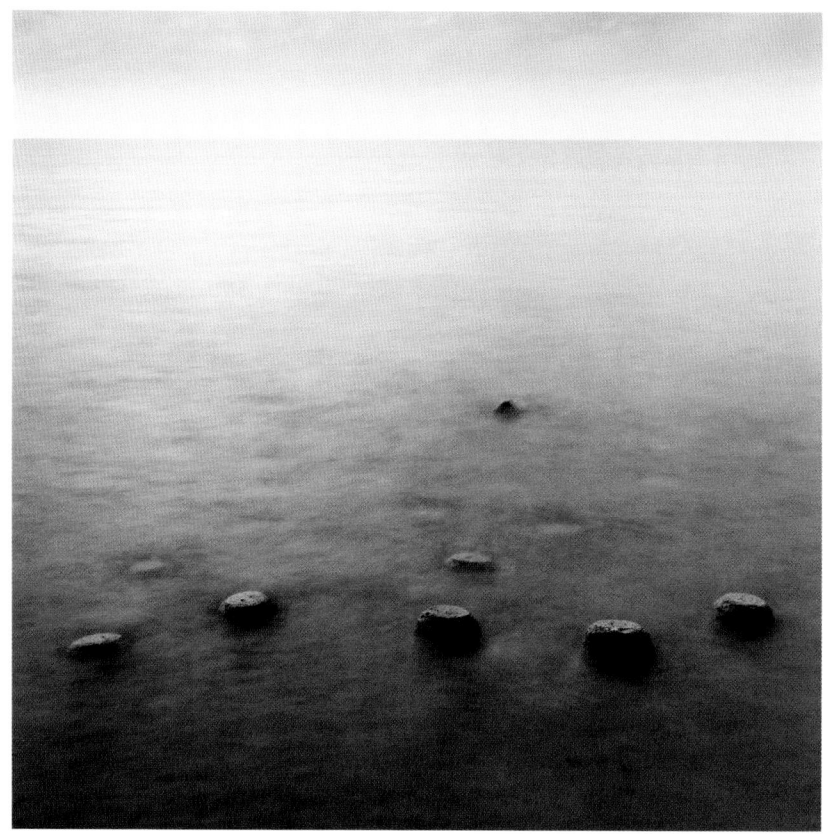

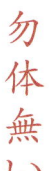 Mottainai

The word originates from the Buddhism term *mottai*, which originally expressed 'the way it should be', and *nai* negates this. *Mottainai* means a feeling of wastefulness. You might hear in this word an injunction not to waste your food in Japan. But this is misuse not just in a narrow, material sense – squandering natural resources, spending extravagantly or 'wasting' your time. It can mean a more spiritual reckoning with the conflicts of disappointment, discomfort and concern that result from feeling you have misdirected your efforts or not achieved your full potential.

Hotoke 仏

In Japanese Buddhism, *hotoke* refers to the spirit of the dead. Every year in the middle of August, family members gather to hold a memorial service (*hōji*) to invite back the spirits of their ancestors. They ask them to spend a few days with their relatives at home. These words point us to a heartfelt tradition of remembrance: your loved ones are always with you and can be called back into heart and home.

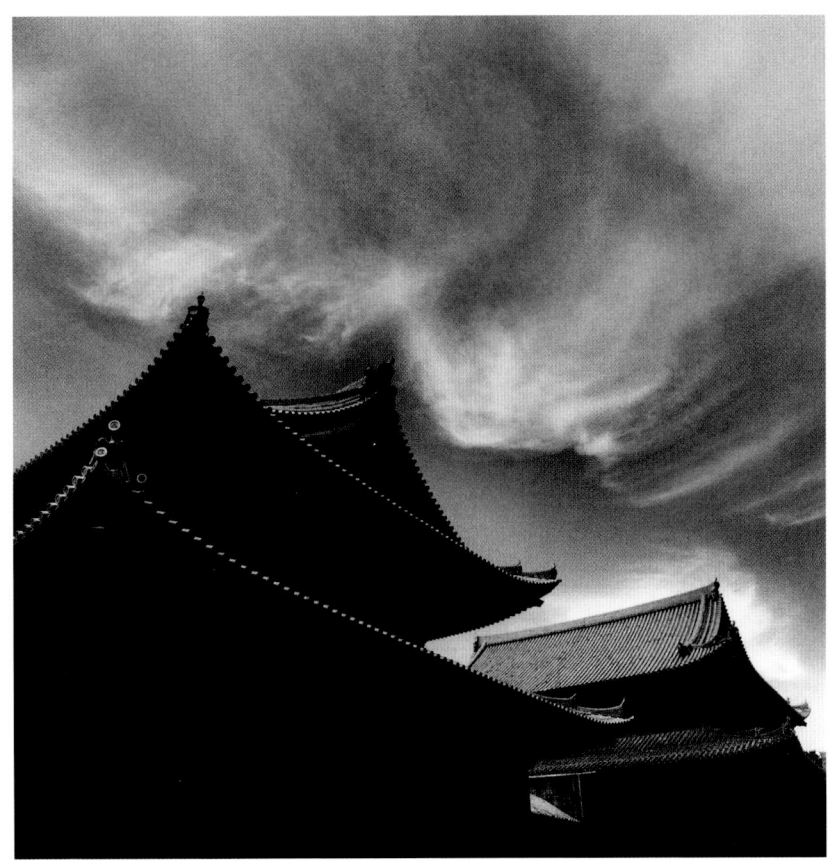

Mari Fujimoto is the Director of Japanese Studies at Queens College, City University of New York where she teaches and lectures in all aspects of Japanese language, linguistics and popular culture. She believes that learning a language is the first step towards understanding the values and beliefs of a culture. Born in Tokyo, she first visited America when she was eight years old and later studied at Queens College for her bachelor's degree and at the Graduate Centre of the City University of New York for her PhD in Linguistics. She now lives in New York with her husband,
fun-loving twins and two dogs.

Michael Kenna is one of the world's leading landscape photographers. His silver gelatin prints have been exhibited in galleries and museums internationally, and are included in many permanent collections such as The Bibliotheque Nationale, Paris; The Metropolitan Museum of Photography, Tokyo; The National Gallery, Washington, D.C.; and the Victoria and Albert Museum, London. Over sixty monographs and exhibition catalogues have been published on his work.

David Buchler is a South African artist living in Tokyo whose artwork engages with contemporary Japanese culture across varied media. He holds a master's degree in Fine Art and collects his meditations, photographs and prints on his blog *Collecting Space*, which he began when he moved to Japan in 2009.

Matsuo Bashō (1644–1694) is remembered today as the great master of the Japanese haiku for his delicate, simple lyrics that capture the natural world in such intensity. The haiku included here are reprinted by permission of Kodansha USA, Inc. Excerpted from *Basho: The Complete Haiku* by Jane Reichhold, copyright © 2008, 2013 by Jane Reichhold.

All the photographs included here are taken from Michael Kenna's Japan collection. Please visit www.michaelkenna.com for more.

pp.2, 95 – Mudra Blessing, Shidoji, Kagawa, Shikoku.
p.3 – Tree Portrait, Study 4, Wakoto, Hokkaido.
p.9 – Kussharo Lake, Study 5, Hokkaido.
p.14 – Mountain Temple, Maegamiji, Ehime, Shikoku.
p.15 – Laughing Buddhas, Otoyo Shrine, Kyoto.
p.23 – Tranquil Morning, Awati Island, Shikoku.
p.24 – Sanskrit Garden, Rengejo-in, Koyasan.
p.32 – Torii in Trees, Wakoto, Hokkaido.
p.36 – Rocky Pier, Tsuda, Shikoku.
p.39 – Pier Fragments, Adogawa, Honshu.
p.45 – Chikui Cape Trees, Muroran, Hokkaido.
p.46 – Autumn Leaves, Unpenji, Shikoku.
p.49 – Sulfer Mountain, Iozan, Hokkaido.
p.50 – Falling Tree, Nagahama, Honshu.
p.53 – Cherry Blossoms, Nara, Honshu.
p.58 – Pier and Nakashima Islands, Toya Lake, Hokkaido.
p.61 – Taushubetsu Bridge, Nukabira, Hokkaido.
p.65 – Butterfly and Peonies, Kongobuji, Koyasan.
p.66 – Buddha statues, Kyoto, Honshu.
p.73 – Donations, Daito Pagoda, Garan, Koyasan.
p.75 – Snowfall, Numakawa, Hokkaido.
p.76 – Torii Gates, Bentendake, Koyasan.
p.81 – Fishing Nets and Mt. Daisen, Yatsuka, Honshu.
p.83 – Frosty Morning, Onuma Lake, Hokkaido.
p.89 – Kussharo Lake, Study 11, Hokkaido.
p.90 – Forest Jizos, Unpenji, Kagawa, Shikoku.
p.101 – Three Bodhisattva's, Osorezan, Honshu.
p.102 – Jizo, Osorezan, Honshu.
p.106 – Posts in Water, Date, Hokkaido.
p.109 – Afternoon Clouds, Myoshi Temple, Kyoto.

Word finder

Amae, 78

Dō, 26, 62, 63, 103

Enryo, 93

Ensō, 25, 56

Fukinsei, 27

Gaman, 94

Go-on, 105

Hanami, 52

Hansei, 82

Hatsu, 88

Heiwa, 21

Hotoke, 108

Ichigo ichie, 88

Ikebana, 26, 27

Ikigai, 59

Isagiyosa, 80

Kaizen, 60

Kanso, 35, 38

Katachi, 64

Kodawari, 67

Kotodama, 77

Misogi, 48

Mono-no aware, 51, 52

Mottainai, 107

Mugon-no gyō, 92

Reigi sahō, 103

Seishin shyūyō, 62, 100

Sensei, 104, 105

Shibui, 37

Shinrinyoku, 47

Shizen, 44

Shōganai, 74

Sunao, 74

Takumi, 64

Teinei, 100

Uchi, 79

Utsukushii, 34

Wa, 20, 21

Acknowledgements

Mari Fujimoto: I would like gratefully to acknowledge Patricia Welch, PhD, Professor of Japanese and Comparative Literature at Hofstra University, for her suggestions in the initial stages of the project; David Buchler, for his thoughtful meditations on Japanese language, beauty and culture, included here; Michael Kenna for granting us permission to reproduce his beautiful photographs alongside my 'words to live by'; and the team at Elwin Street Productions, for conceiving of and supporting the project from beginning to completion.

David Buchler: Thank you to my friends and family, here in Japan and in South Africa, especially my sister, Louise, for constantly inspiring me to write; to Koichi for always encouraging me to create and stay strong; and to Tokyo, for just being incredible and for showing me something new every day.